P9-EIE-454
59

THE ECONOMIC ORIGINS OF THE FRENCH REVOLUTION

Poverty or Prosperity?

PROBLEMS IN EUROPEAN CIVILIZATION

UNDER THE EDITORIAL DIRECTION OF

Ralph W. Greenlaw

THE PIRENNE THESIS — ANALYSIS, CRITICISM, AND REVISION

THE CORONATION OF CHARLEMAGNE — WHAT DID IT SIGNIFY?

THE RENAISSANCE — MEDIEVAL OR MODERN?

MACHIAVELLI — CYNIC, PATRIOT, OR POLITICAL SCIENTIST?

PROTESTANTISM AND CAPITALISM — THE WEBER THESIS AND ITS CRITICS

THE ORIGINS OF THE ENGLISH CIVIL WAR — CONSPIRACY, CRUSADE, OR CLASS CONFLICT?

THE GREATNESS OF LOUIS XIV — MYTH OR REALITY?

THE ECONOMIC ORIGINS OF THE FRENCH REVOLUTION — POVERTY OR PROSPERITY?

THE INDUSTRIAL REVOLUTION IN BRITAIN — TRIUMPH OR DISASTER?

1848 — A TURNING POINT?

THE "NEW IMPERIALISM" — ANALYSIS OF LATE NINETEENTH-CENTURY EXPANSION

THE OUTBREAK OF THE FIRST WORLD WAR — WHO WAS RESPONSIBLE?

THE RUSSIAN REVOLUTION AND BOLSHEVIK VICTORY — WHY AND HOW?

THE VERSAILLES SETTLEMENT — WAS IT FOREDOOMED TO FAILURE?

THE ETHIOPIAN CRISIS — TOUCHSTONE OF APPEASEMENT?

THE NAZI REVOLUTION — GERMANY'S GUILT OR GERMANY'S FATE?

Other volumes in preparation

THE ECONOMIC ORIGINS OF THE FRENCH REVOLUTION

Poverty or Prosperity?

EDITED WITH AN INTRODUCTION BY

Ralph W. Greenlaw, WELLESLEY COLLEGE

D. C. HEATH AND COMPANY · BOSTON

Library of Congress Catalog Card number 58-12571

PRINTED IN THE UNITED STATES OF AMERICA

Table of Contents

Introduction

In the summer of 1789, at about the same time that the citizens of Paris were assuring the victory of the Third Estate and the successful establishment of the National Assembly by resorting to violence on July 14, the peasants of France were initiating a rebellion of their own directed against their seigneurs and the vestiges of the feudal regime. Limited in some instances to a mere passive refusal to pay their traditional seigneurial obligations, in others it flared into physical violence directed against the seigneur or his property with the ultimate aim in most cases being the destruction of the *terriers* or legal documents on which their seigneurial obligations were recorded. There is evidence that in many areas the peasant masses were incited to this action by a wave of mass hysteria known as the "Great Fear" which arose in reaction to the rumored existence of an "aristocratic conspiracy" directed against the people, who, it was alleged, were to be physically coerced into submission by bands of hired brigands. When, by the end of July, the National Assembly at Versailles became aware of the extent of rural disaffection, it found itself compelled either to use armed force to restore order or to accept the peasants' actions as a *fait accompli.* Since the only forces available were royal troops which might easily be turned against the Assembly itself, the only course open to the deputies was to legalize the existing situation. This was done on the famous night of August 4, 1789, when the Assembly by a series of resolutions virtually destroyed the feudal regime in France. Besides being perhaps the single most revolutionary act of the Assembly during its entire career, it was also one of its most permanent. No subsequent government of the Revolutionary or Restoration eras, even at the height of reaction, felt strong enough to reverse this action.

Because the peasants played such an important role in the events of 1789, the question of their motives becomes one of primary importance in any discussion of the origins of the Revolution. Along with the "Great Fear" which has already been mentioned, the immediate cause of their action was unquestionably the general revolutionary ferment and the resulting anarchy which swept over France during the spring and summer of 1789. But what were the more basic underlying causes which determined the character and objectives of their action? We know that political and ideological factors played an important role in bringing on the French Revolution, but what was the part played by economic considerations? Did the people have economic as well as political grievances, and, if so, what were they? Did these grievances stem from a condition of grinding poverty or from one of gradually rising prosperity which only made the lower classes more dissatisfied with their lot? Just what was the economic condition of the people of France during the 18th century, and especially what was the condition of the peasant class to which the vast majority of the French people belonged? These are the questions on which the following selected readings focus and to which they give a variety of answers for the reader to consider.

The first selection is from the Introduction to Michelet's history of the Revolution published in 1847. It sets forth what might now be described as the traditional view on this question, which is that the Revolution stemmed in very large measure from the misery of the oppressed classes, both rural and urban. Although to Michelet it was fundamentally a revolt made in the name of freedom against tyranny, it is clear that one reason he approved of it was because he felt that for the masses the Old Regime had meant only unrelieved want and poverty. In large part this misery had its origin in the ruinous and oppressive fiscal policy followed by a greedy and corrupt royal government which ground the faces of its defenseless subjects into the earth. Apart from the crushing burdens imposed by the government, the misery also stemmed from the iniquitous social and economic system which put the peasant at the mercy of the exploiting and usually absent seigneur. The tones and colors of the outraged and indignant Michelet blend together to produce a picture which is at best somber and at worst full of dark, foreboding hues. Michelet was not the first writer to describe the condition of the people in these terms. It had been so described by most of the writers who up until his time had tried to defend or justify the Revolution, but the power of his romantic imagination and his purple prose, perhaps more than anything else, helped to establish this picture as the stereotype. Modern American students are probably most likely to have become acquainted with it through the medium of Dickens' *A Tale of Two Cities.*

Although Michelet both in time and temperament falls into what might be called the romantic school of historical writing, he prided himself on being a careful practitioner of the historian's craft. Perhaps because of a romantic's desire to know and actually recreate a segment of the past he carried on extensive research in the archives and always insisted that he maintained a rigorously critical attitude toward his sources. But although he boasted of having spent eight years in the research and writing of his seven-volume work, he seemingly did not spend a relatively great amount of this time studying conditions under the Old Regime. The discussion of these was limited to a fifty-page introduction in which he traced in summary fashion the history of the French monarchy over the preceding five centuries. Very probably he did not devote more time and space to this topic because it never occurred to him that an unprejudiced person would raise any questions about the view of it which he presented. He was much more concerned with *how* the French people had won their freedom; the question of why they wanted it would probably have seemed to him pointless.

Three years after the appearance of the last of Michelet's volumes in 1853, a work was published which directly challenged a great many of his affirmations about social and economic conditions during the 18th century. This new book was written by the eminent political and social philosopher and writer, Alexis de Tocqueville. Tocqueville had made a name for himself as a keen sociological observer and analyst as a result of the brilliant success of his *Democracy in America,* and he had played a prominent role in political life both before and after the Revolution of 1848. He served briefly as foreign minister during the Second Republic and went into enforced retirement, a bitter and disillusioned man, after the *coup d'etat* of Louis Napoleon in 1851. A desire to try to understand the reasons for the violent and unstable tenor of French political life as he had himself experienced it during the first half of the 19th century impelled him to turn to a study of the Old Regime and the Revolution from which the France he knew had emerged. The fruit of this effort was the volume entitled *L'ancien régime et la révolution française* which was meant to be only the first part of a large scale study, but death overtook him just as he was embarking on his study of the Revolutionary era itself. As a result, this volume, in spite of its title, was limited to an analysis of the Old Regime. It was based on exhaustive research in many of the provincial archives.

One complete chapter and a portion of another from this volume constitute the second selection in this collection of readings. These portions have been selected because in them Tocqueville addressed himself directly to the question of the condition and situation of the peasant under the Old Regime. The divergence between his view and that of Michelet's is manifest almost at the outset when Tocqueville asserts flatly that whatever may have been the condition of the French peasant according to any absolute standard, he is certain that the tiller of the soil in France was better off than the peasant of any other country in Europe. He stresses that unlike the peasant-serf of eastern Europe, the French peasant was, except in a small area in the Franche-Comté, a free man, and unlike the English tenant farmer was also in many instances a landowner. He also suggests that although the few seigneurial monetary obligations that remained in the 18th century were greatly resented, nevertheless they did not constitute a serious financial burden. In total, and at almost every point, the contrast between the views of Tocqueville and Michelet is direct and striking.

In spite of Tocqueville's work, however, the view of Michelet seemed to hold the field. In the preface written for a new edition of his history in 1868, Michelet mentioned the names of several critics of his work, but did not include Tocqueville's among them – perhaps because the latter's one volume had a bearing on only a relatively tiny portion of Michelet's seven volumes. In any case, it was Michelet's picture of social and economic conditions under the Old Regime that received impressive reenforcement with the publication of H. Taine's study of the Old Regime which appeared in 1875. One chapter from this volume makes up the third selection which follows. Taine, who had already made a name as a professor of literature and a philosopher, had, like Tocqueville, been drawn to the study and writing of history by events which he had seen taking place before his very eyes. In this instance it was the defeat of 1870, the German occupation, and above all the Commune of 1871 which furnished the compulsive force. It was the latter which convinced Taine that Frenchmen had to be made to see the evil and futility of all revolutions. This meant that the myth of the glorious days of 1789–1794 had to be destroyed and to this end Taine turned all his scholarly and literary powers. Realizing that any adequate account of the Revolution had to begin with a discussion of the Old Regime, he plunged into the archives in order to learn for himself all that he could about it. The initial result of this effort was the work mentioned above. The picture of the Old Regime which emerged from the pages of Taine turned out to be much closer to Michelet's than to Tocqueville's. Unlike Tocqueville he found in that epoch a condition of widespread misery and degradation very similar to that already so strikingly depicted by Michelet. With an impressive mastery of detail he added, bit by bit, a massive array of evidence based on archival materials which helped to make the indictment more effective than ever. But, where Michelet had seen these conditions as more than adequate justification for violent revolution when the opportunity presented itself, Taine, on the other hand, in this and subsequent volumes both directly and by implication, unequivocally condemned the Revolution and the violent means by which it had been accomplished. To him it had meant disaster for France and far from liberating Frenchmen in any real sense, he felt that its only effects had been to deliver them over for a time to their basest passions and to mislead them as to how true prosperity and happiness could be obtained. The evil conditions on the eve of the Revolution which he described with such an impressive wealth of detail went a long way toward explaining the crudeness and brutality as well as the overwhelming power of the forces which were unleashed. Whereas to Michelet the "great days" of the Revolution were always the work of the true hero of the Revolution, the "people," to Taine they were the work of "the mob," the *canaille*. For Taine any political or social system which opened the way to its domination could result only in evils of the kind which he himself had witnessed during the dark days of the Commune of 1871. The anti-democratic lesson which he intended for his contemporaries was too obvious to be missed.

In spite of Taine's warning against "popular" movements, the Third Republic managed somehow to survive and inevitably found its defenders. One of the most famous of these was Alphonse Aulard, distinguished historian of the Revolution and first incumbent of the Chair of French Revolutionary History established at the University of Paris in 1885. Aulard defended the Third Republic by undertaking to justify the First French Republic which was its ideological forebear. This meant that the view of the Revolution elaborated by Taine had in some way to be countered. Aulard was primarily a political historian and devoted his major efforts to defending the political ideology of the Revolution, but in the course of his annual lectures at the University he touched on almost all phases of its history. Since Taine had described and condemned the crude and bestial violence of the popular movement which he had seen as arising from the inhuman conditions which prevailed before 1789, it is not surprising that Aulard attempted to soften this picture. In refuting Taine (he devoted one whole book to that subject alone) he tried to show how relatively few were the actual outbreaks of violence in 1789, at least those which could be adequately documented, and argued that in most respects Taine's picture of conditions under the Old Regime was somewhat overdrawn. The selection from Aulard is not taken from his book against Taine, but it follows the same general line of argument. It deals specifically with the question of the degree of oppressiveness of the so-called feudal obligations in the years immediately preceding the upheaval of 1789. As will be seen in several of the selections this question of whether seigneurial rights were becoming more burdensome during the reign of Louis XVI is one of the important issues in this general problem. Aulard's conclusion is that there is insufficient evidence to support a positive affirmation that these were becoming more burdensome. This would tend to support his view that conditions under the Old Regime were not so bad as to make the peasants strike out blindly and violently as Taine had alleged.

Although Aulard challenged Taine's view of the Revolution both in general and in particulars, including the question of conditions under the Old Regime, the most direct challenge to Michelet's and Taine's views on this question came from the group of Marxist historians which became prominent at the beginning of the 20th century. According to Marxist dogma the Revolution was brought about by a wealthy, confident bourgeois class which having effectively taken over economic power as a result of the rise of capitalism, then wished to extend its dominance to the political and social sphere where it found its ambitions thwarted by the outmoded political, social, and economic structure of the Old Regime. In their view, the Revolution was the work of a class on the rise; a class which had so strengthened its economic position and power during the course of the century that it could no longer be denied. Accordingly the picture of poverty, misery, and economic distress that had been drawn by Michelet and Taine had to be revised. This task was undertaken initially by the socialist political leader of the turn of the century, Jean Jaurès. In his *Histoire Socialiste de la Révolution Française,* published in 1900, he spelled out at length and in considerable detail the evidence for the growth of wealth and prosperity in France during the course of the 18th century. To be sure, all elements of the Third Estate had not participated in or benefited from this prosperity equally, but Jaurès' view of the situation of the peasantry was much closer to that of Tocqueville than to that of either Michelet or Taine. Jaurès' arguments and proofs are too long and detailed to be reproduced here, but the main burden of his thesis was adopted by the materialist historians who followed him and most notably by the great Revolutionary scholar, Albert Mathiez. Whereas Jaurès was an historian by avocation, Mathiez was a professional, and during a long and productive career which covered the first three decades of the 20th century, Mathiez expanded and elaborated on Jaurès' ideas at almost every point. Although much of Mathiez's work concentrated on the Revolution itself and especially the Terror, nevertheless in his short, general history of the Revolution published in the 1920's Mathiez dealt briefly with conditions under the Old Regime and followed in almost every respect the line of argument suggested by Jaurès. A very brief excerpt which suggests Mathiez's general view is here presented as the fifth selection.

At this point it might seem that views on the question had arrived at a stand-off, but there is another strain of opinion which has not been mentioned. Almost from the time of the Revolution itself there were anti-Revolutionary and pro-Royalist writers who condemned the Revolution in almost its every aspect. For the most part these adopted the argument that although unquestionably some evils had existed under the Old Regime, on the whole these had been exaggerated by the Revolutionaries themselves and by historians sympathetic to their cause. The writers in this hostile tradition generally went on to argue that the old order was basically sound in every way and would have required only a little tinkering to repair a few obvious faults. This was a view which found support in the work of Tocqueville, and more ironically in that of the Marxist historians—ironically, because the Marxists obviously believed, in conformity to their principles of economic determinism, that it was the prosperous condition of the bourgeoisie in the 18th century which had made the Revolution both possible and inevitable. But if conditions had not been so bad under the Old Regime and misery and distress not endemic, then obviously to some it would seem that there had been little need for violent revolution. Research by some of these conservative historians along lines first opened up by Tocqueville led to an impressive massing of evidence in support of the view that conditions in the 18th century French countryside were idyllic in comparison to the harsh, individualistic bourgeois world of the 19th and 20th centuries. M. Frantz Funck-Brentano, a modern, and in some quarters, highly respected French historian, just before the first World War, published a study of the Old Regime which, with an obvious feeling of nostalgia, paints such an idyllic picture. He marshalls a considerable amount of evidence from primary sources to show that many of the evils which allegedly existed under the Old Regime when examined closely or put in their proper perspective turn out not to have been so bad after all. A brief excerpt from this work relating to the condition of the peasantry constitutes the sixth selection.

Just as the radical Paris Commune of 1871 generated the anti-Revolutionary tract of Taine, so the Communist threat in the 20th century has generated a new breed of anti-Revolutionary historians who see the Reds of the 20th century as the lineal descendants of the Jacobins of 1794. And this is no self-induced figment of the imagination—the Communists themselves claim Robespierre's to have been the first attempt to establish a socialist dictatorship (this was Mathiez's view though he was not himself a Communist). Accordingly at least one 20th-century historian, Pierre Gaxotte, has attempted to attack Communism by again attacking and condemning the Revolution of 1789. With new ammunition he refurbishes the old anti-Revolutionary viewpoint which looked on the Revolution as an unprovoked and unnecessary disaster from beginning to end. In a work on the Revolution published in the 1920's and which had a tremendous popular sale, Gaxotte affirmed that on the whole conditions even for the lowest classes were not intolerable under the Old Regime and that a few minor readjustments could have kept it viable. Again the irony of the situation is evident because in presenting his arguments he relies most heavily on the work of Jaurés and Mathiez and uses their evidence, not to show why the Revolution inevitably came, but rather to argue that if economic conditions were so favorable then there was no need for violent revolution. This is one of the neatest examples available to illustrate how the same basic historical data can be used to support diametrically opposite conclusions. The portion of Gaxotte's work giving his view of conditions during the last years of the monarchy makes up the seventh selection.

One of the great contributions which Mathiez and the Marxist school has made to our knowledge and understanding of the Revolution has been in its emphasis on the need for detailed reseach on social and economic aspects of the Revolution at the most basic level. In this area Mathiez himself was a pioneer and he inspired a whole generation of scholars to carry on this kind of work. But, as indicated above, Mathiez was not primarily interested in the Old Regime and his conclusions in this area were built largely on the work of Jaurès. By the 1920's it had become apparent that little or no further progress on the question of the actual economic state of the people in France on the eve of 1789 could be made until a great deal more basic research had been accomplished.

Much pioneering work on questions of the division of land and modes of land tenure in 18th-century France had been done by several Russian scholars before the first World War. The material turned up by them and a few other scholars working in that field was used by the economic historian, Henri Sée, to compile a short study of social and economic conditions in France in the 18th century which he published in 1925. Sée's book tried to hold to a rather judicious middle line between Jaurés' tableau of prosperity and Taine's sketch of peasant misery although the new evidence he presents seems to favor the former somewhat more than the latter. Sée's work is especially valuable because it gets beyond the level of generalities which is characteristic of all the selections presented up to this point and applies itself to specific questions such as the proportion of land held by the various classes, the size of holdings, the wages of laborers, etc.

As the study of economic history has become more "scientific" it has become evident that the general economic condition of a nation, or a class, is not determined by a few simple factors, but rather by a vast complex of interacting factors such as prices, wages (real and nominal), rents, degree of industrialization, modes of production, etc. Logically the next step, therefore, was for the economic historian of the Old Regime to try to develop reliable data on these many complex items. A pioneering venture of this kind was undertaken in the late 20's by another French scholar, C. E. Labrousse, who set out to make a detailed study of the movement of the prices and incomes in France during the 18th century. The results of this study were published in 1932. They were based on exhaustive and detailed research at both the local and national level. Although he concentrated on price and income data, Labrousse also brought in other economic data where it was available and pertinent. He then proceeded to interpret it in most effective and illuminating fashion.

Continuing his studies along these lines Labrousse published a second volume in 1943 in which he focused his attention on what he called the crisis of the economy at the end of the Old Regime and the beginning of the Revolution. In this work he addressed himself more directly to the problem of the relationship of economic conditions during the reign of Louis XVI to the outbreak of revolution in 1789. As a result of both of these exhaustive studies M. Labrousse came to a conclusion which seems to stand midway between that of

Michelet and that of Jaurès, although perhaps closer to the former than the latter. In his introduction to this second work M. Labrousse summarizes his conclusions as to the effect of economic conditions in 18th-century France on the outbreak of the Revolution, and the major portion of this summary makes up the ninth selection.

At this point perhaps a word of warning is in order. One might well feel tempted to accept Labrousse's views as the last word on the subject because his scientific approach and impressive use of statistical data make his arguments seem extremely compelling. But do the economic facts and figures as revealed in his charts and tables (these underlie all his conclusions, although none are included in the selection from his work which follows) give us a more accurate picture of economic conditions at the level of daily living and people's reaction to them, than do the accounts of conscientious and perceptive scholars using more traditional sources? Should the evidence of Michelet, Taine, Tocqueville and others be disregarded because it is not based on statistical tables and trend curves? One should perhaps guard against being dazzled by the glitter of a "scientific" apparatus and be cautious about accepting its assumptions and conclusions too uncritically. All quantitative data bearing on a complex historical problem of cause and effect must be interpreted in terms of its qualitative or "human effect," and wherever interpretation is necessary it is possible for disagreement to arise.

About the same time as Labrousse was working on his study of wages and prices, another prominent French scholar of the Revolution, Georges Lefebvre published a detailed study of the social and economic history of a single Department in the north of France just prior to and during the Revolution. Whereas Labrousse approached his study of the economy of the Old Regime by abstracting a limited number of what he considered to be crucial economic factors and attempting to study their movement on a nation-wide scale, Lefebvre preferred to follow the alternative method of limiting himself to a small geographical area and studying its society and economy in its totality and in all its variegated detail. This study has given Lefebvre an incomparable grasp of the intricacies and complexities of the economic life of 18th-century France, and the volume which he published is a masterpiece of analysis and interpretation. Since this major work does not lend itself to excerpting, Lefebvre's views on the problem at hand are set forth in an extract from an article which he published in 1932 dealing with the general question of the peasants and the Revolution. This makes up the tenth selection. It is a particularly important one because in it Lefebvre, who is considered by many to be the foremost living authority on the subject, emphasizes those factors which particularly influenced peasant attitudes toward the whole Revolutionary movement, and shows the divergence between peasant and bourgeois viewpoints.

Unlike Labrousse who admits to holding a position midway between Michelet and Jaurès on the issue of poverty or prosperity as a cause of the Revolution, Lefebvre, while recognizing the general rising level of prosperity during the century, seems to put much more emphasis on the basic poverty and insecurity of the peasant masses. He stresses peasant hostility toward the introduction of capitalistic ideas and techniques into agriculture and emphasizes the fragility of the alliance between the peasant and the bourgeois landholder against their common enemy, the seigneur. Although Lefebvre does not mention it in the excerpt included here, he does stand in complete agreement with Labrousse on the point that the economic crisis of 1788–9 was crucial in producing a state of mind receptive to the idea of revolutionary action in the lower classes of both city and country. It should also be noted that with both Labrousse and Lefebvre the marked partisanship which has been noted as characteristic of earlier writers has largely disappeared. In the controversy as to the relative importance of poverty or prosperity they both maintain an independent middle position.

The last selection is included not because it has any particularly original contribution to make toward the solution of the problem, but it does present the conclusions reached by an experienced, mature scholar. It is especially interesting to note the particular points which the writer has chosen to emphasize or ignore. The author, Frédéric Braesch, in years past was a specialist on certain financial aspects of the Revolution. Like Tocqueville and Taine he was turned to a consideration of the general meaning and significance of the Revolution by a disaster which his country experienced during his own lifetime – the humiliating defeat by Hitler in 1940. M. Braesch felt that the Revolution had indeed been the crucial event of modern French history and out of the whole period he felt that the very first year, 1789, had been the crucial year. His book is, therefore, a detailed study of the events of that year and of the conditions of the Old Regime that produced them. It is the latter which is of immediate interest for us and it is a part of this portion of his work which is presented here.

Careful study of the following selections will probably make it evident that in order to work his way through the mass of detail and reduce his views to some kind of order, the student must arrive at some opinion of his own as to what are the decisive elements in the formation of people's aims and attitudes and what are the crucial economic considerations which might compel men to undertake or accept violent change in government or society. In this sense the problem although concerned with one aspect of a particular historical era is timeless in its relevance.

The Conflict of Opinion

"Not only does the land produce less, but it is less cultivated. In many places it is not worth while to cultivate it. Large proprietors tired of advancing to their peasants sums that never return, neglect the land which would require expensive improvements. The portion cultivated grows less and the desert expands. . . . How can we be surprised that the crops should fail with such half-starved husbandmen, or that the land should suffer and refuse to yield? The yearly produce no longer suffices for the year. As we approach 1789, Nature yields less and less."

— JULES MICHELET

"At first sight it seems hard to account for this steady increase in the wealth of the country despite the as yet unremedied shortcomings of the administration and the obstacles with which industry still had to contend. . . . That France could prosper and grow rich, given the inequality of taxation, the vagaries of local laws, internal customs barriers, feudal rights, the trade corporations, the sales of offices and all the rest, may well seem hardly credible. Yet the fact remains that the country did grow richer and living conditions improved throughout the land."

— ALEXIS DE TOCQUEVILLE

"Examine administrative correspondence for the last thirty years preceding the Revolution. Countless statements reveal excessive suffering, even when not terminating in fury. Life to a man of the lower class, to an artisan, or workman, subsisting on the labor of his own hands, is evidently precarious; he obtains simply enough to keep him from starvation and he does not always get that."

— HIPPOLYTE TAINE

"An infallible sign that the wealth of the country was increasing was that the population was growing rapidly and the prices of commodities, land, and houses were steadily rising. . . . Comfort was gradually spreading downwards, from the upper to the lower middle class and that of artisans and small shopkeepers. People dressed better and had better food than in former days. . . . And so the Revolution was not to break out in an exhausted country but, on the contrary, in a flourishing land on a rising tide of progress. Poverty may sometimes lead to riots, but it cannot bring about great social upheavals. These always arise from a disturbance of the balance between the classes."

— ALBERT MATHIEZ

"The Revolution indeed appears in many respects as it did to Michelet, and in contradiction to the ideas of Jaurès as later taken up by Mathiez, to have been a revolution stemming from misery. Not that Jaurès and Mathiez denied the reality and the influence of misery, but according to them it played only a minor and incidental role."

— C. E. LABROUSSE

FAMINE IN THE EIGHTEENTH CENTURY

JULES MICHELET

Born in 1798 and one of France's most celebrated historians of the 19th century, Michelet was probably most renowned for his nineteen-volume history of France. The romantic era in which he lived inevitably conditioned both his viewpoint and his style. A sincere though temperate republican he had the typical romantic's belief in the People, and the story of their patience, fortitude, and instinctive virtue constitutes the major theme of his history of the French Revolution, from which the following excerpt is taken.

I WILL presently investigate the idea on which France subsisted – the government of grace and paternal monarchy; that inquiry will be much promoted perhaps, if I first establish, by authentic proofs, the results in which this system had at length terminated. A tree is known by its fruits.

First, nobody will deny that it secured for this people the glory of a prodigious and incredible patience. Read the foreign travellers of the last two centuries; you behold them stupefied, when travelling through our plains, at their wretched appearance, at the sadness, the solitude, the miserable poverty, the dismal, naked, empty cottages, and the starving, ragged population. There they learn what man is able to endure without dying; what nobody, neither the English, the Dutch, nor the Germans, would have supported.

What astonishes them still more, is the resignation of this people, their respect for their masters, lay or ecclesiastical, and their idolatrous attachment for their kings. That they should preserve, amid such sufferings, so much patience and meekness, such goodness and docility, so little rancour for oppression, is indeed a strange mystery. It perhaps explains itself partly by the kind of careless philosophy, the too indifferent facility with which the Frenchman welcomes bad weather; it will be fine again sooner or later; rain today, sunshine tomorrow. He does not grumble at a rainy day.

French sobriety also, that eminently military quality, aided their resignation. Our soldiers, in this matter, as in every other, have shown the limits of human endurance. Their fasting, in painful marches and excessive toils, would have frightened the lazy hermits of the Thebais, such as Anthony and Pachomus.

We must learn from Marshall Villars how the armies of Louis XIV used to live; "Several times we thought that bread would absolutely fail us; then, by great efforts, we got together enough for half a day; the next day is got over by fasting. When M. d'Artagnan marched, the brigades not marching were obliged to fast. Our sustenance is a miracle, and the virtue and firmness of our soldiers are marvellous. *Panem nostrum quotidianum da nobis hobiè* ["Give us this day our daily bread"], say they to me as I pass through the ranks, after they have but the quarter and the half ration.

From *Historical View of the French Revolution,* translated by C. Cocks from Jules Michelet, *Histoire de la Révolution française* (Paris, 1879), Introduction, Section II, pp. 38–42. By permission of George Bell & Sons, London.

I encourage them and give them promises; they merely shrug up their shoulders, and gaze at me with a look of resignation that affects me. 'The Marshall is right,' say they; 'we must learn to suffer sometimes.'"

Patience! Virtue! Resignation! Can any one help being affected, on meeting with such traces of the goodness of our fathers?

Who will enable me to go through the history of their long sufferings, their gentleness and moderation? It was long the astonishment, sometimes the laughing-stock of Europe! Great merriment was it for the English to see those soldiers half-starved and almost naked, yet cheerful, amiable, and good towards their officers; performing, without a murmur, immense marches, and, if they found nothing in the evening, making their supper of songs.

If patience merits heaven, this people, in the two last centuries, truly surpassed all the merits of the saints; but how shall we make the legend? Their vestiges are widely diffused. Misery is a general fact; the virtue to support it a virtue so common among us, that historians seldom deign to notice it. Moreover, history is defective in the eighteenth century; France, after the cruel fatigues of the wars of Louis XIV, suffers too much to relate her own story. No more memoirs; nobody has the courage to write his individual life; even vanity is mute, having but shame to tell. Till the philosophical movement, this country is silent – like the deserted palace of Louis XIV – surviving his own family, like the chamber of the dying man who still governs, the old Cardinal Fleury.

It is difficult to describe properly the history of those times, as they are unmarked by rebellions. No people ever had fewer. This nation loved her masters; she had no rebellion – nothing but a Revolution.

It is from their very masters, their kings, princes, ministers, prelates, magistrates, and intendants, that we may learn to what extremities the people were reduced. It is they who are about to describe the restraints in which the people were held.

The mournful procession in which they all advance one after the other in order to recount the death of France, is led by Colbert in 1681: "One can go on no longer," says he, and he dies. They do go on however, for they expel half a million of industrious men about 1685, and kill still more, in a thirty years' war. But, good God! how many more die of misery!

As early as 1698, the result is visible. The intendants themselves, who create the evil, reveal and deplore it. In the memorials which they are asked to give for the young duke of Burgundy, they declare that such a province has lost the quarter of its inhabitants, another a third, and another the half. And the population is not renewed; the peasant is so miserable that his children are all weak, sickly, and unable to live.

Let us follow attentively the series of years. That deplorable period of 1698 becomes an object of regret. "Then," says Boisguillebert, a magistrate, "there was still oil in the lamp. Today (1707) it goes out for want of nourishment" – A mournful expression; and he adds a threatening sentence; one would think it was the year '89: "The trial will now be between those who pay, and those whose only function is to receive."

The preceptor to the grandson of Louis XIV, the Archbishop of Cambrai, is not less *revolutionnaire* than this petty Norman magistrate: "The people no longer live like men; it is no longer safe to rely upon their patience. The old machine will break up at the first shock. We dare not look upon the state of exhaustion which we have now attained; all we can do is to shut our eyes, open our hands, and go on taking."

Louis XIV dies at last, and the people thank God. Happily we have the regent, that good duke of Orleans, who, if Fenelon still lived, would take him for his counsellor; he prints *Telemachus;* France shall be a Salentum. No more wars. We are now the friends of England; we give up to her our commerce, our honour, nay even our State secrets. Who would believe that, in the bosom of peace, this aimable prince, in only seven years, finds means to add to the two billions and a half of debts left by Louis XIV, *seven hundred and fifty millions* (of francs) more? – The whole paid up in paper.

"If I were a subject," he used to say, "I would most certainly revolt." And when he was told that a disturbance was about to take place, "The people are right," said he; "they are goodnatured fools to suffer so long!"

Fleury is as economical as the regent was lavish. Does France improve? I doubt it, when I see that the bread presented to Louis XV as the bread that the people ate, is bread made of fern.

The Bishop of Chartres told him, that, in his diocese, the men browsed with the sheep. What is perhaps still stronger, is, that M. d'Argenson (a minister) speaking of the sufferings of those times, contrasts them with *the good time*. Guess which. That of the regent and the duke – the time when France, exhausted by Louis XIV, and bleeding at every pore, sought a remedy in a bankruptcy of three billions!

Everybody sees the crisis approaching. Fenelon says, so early as 1709: "The old machine will break up at the first shock." It does not break up yet. Then Madame de Chateauroux, about 1742: "I see plainly that there will be a general overthrow, if no remedy be used." Yes, Madam, everybody sees it – the king and your successor, Madame de Pompadour, as well as the economists, the philosophers, foreigners, everybody. All admire the longanimity of this people; it is Job sitting among the nations. O meekness! O patience! – Walpole laughs at it, but I mourn over it. That unfortunate people still loves; still believes; is obstinate in hoping. It is ever waiting for its saviour. Which? Its God-man, its king.

Ridiculous yet affecting idolatry – What will this God, this king, do? He possesses neither the firm will, nor the power, perhaps, to cure the deeply-rooted, inveterate, universal evil now consuming, parching, famishing the community, draining its life's blood from its veins – from its very heart.

The evil consists in this, that the nation, from the highest to the lowest, is organised so as to go on producing less and less, and paying more and more. She will go on declining, wasting away, giving, after her blood, her marrow; and there will be no end to it, till having reached the last gasp, and just expiring, the convulsion of the death-struggle arouses her once more and raises that pale feeble body on its legs – Feeble? – grown strong perhaps by fury!

Let us minutely examine, if you will, these words *producing less and less*. They are exact to the letter.

As early as under Louis XIV the excise (*aides*) already weighed so heavily, that at Mantes, Etampes, and elsewhere, all the vines were plucked up.

The peasant having no goods to seize, the exchequer can lay hold of nothing but the cattle; it is gradually exterminated. No more manure. The cultivation of corn, though extended in the seventeenth century, by immense clearings of waste land, decreases in the eighteenth. The earth can no longer repair her generative strength; she fasts, and becomes exhausted; as the cattle may become extinct, so also the land now appears dead.

Not only does the land produce less, but it is less cultivated. In many places, it is not worth while to cultivate it. Large proprietors tired of advancing to their peasants sums that never return, neglect the land which would require expensive improvements. The portion cultivated grows less, and the desert expands. People talk of agriculture, write books on it, make expensive experiments, paradoxical schemes of cultivation; and agriculture, devoid of succour, of cattle, grows wild. Men, women, and children yoke themselves to the plough. They would dig the ground with their nails if our ancient laws did not, at least, defend the plough share – the last poor implement that furrows the earth. How can we be surprised that the crops should fail with such half-starved husbandmen, or that the land should suffer and refuse to yield? The yearly produce no longer suffices for the year. As we approach

1789, Nature yields less and less. Like a beast over fatigued, unwilling to move one step further, and preferring to lie down and die, she waits, and produces no more. Liberty is not only the life of man, but also that of nature.

FEUDALISM IN EIGHTEENTH CENTURY FRANCE

ALEXIS DE TOCQUEVILLE

Alexis de Tocqueville, a Frenchman of aristocratic background born in 1805, is best known to Americans for his brilliant analysis of American democracy in the 1830's. Disillusioned and excluded from active political life by Louis Napoleon's coup d'état of 1851, he devoted his remaining years to a study of the Old Regime in France, hoping to discover in her past the reasons for the vagaries of her political life in the first half of the 19th century. The book which he published in 1856 after many years of research in the local archives is still considered by many scholars to be the best study of the Old Regime available. The following selection is made up of two excerpts from this celebrated work.

Why feudalism had come to be more detested in France than in any other country

At first sight it may appear surprising that the Revolution, whose primary aim, as we have seen, was to destroy every vestige of the institutions of the Middle Ages, should not have broken out in countries where those institutions had the greatest hold and bore most heavily on the people instead of those in which their yoke was relatively light.

At the close of the eighteenth century serfdom had not yet been completely abolished anywhere in Germany; indeed, in most parts of that country the peasants were still literally bound to the land, as they had been in the Middle Ages. The armies of Frederick II and Maria Theresa were composed almost entirely of men who were serfs on the medieval pattern.

In most German states in 1788 the peasant was not allowed to quit his lord's estate; if he did so, he was liable to be tracked down wherever he was and brought back in custody. He was subject to the jurisdiction of his lord, who kept a close eye on his private life and could punish him for intemperance or idleness. He could neither better his social position, change his occupation, nor even marry without his master's consent, and a great number of his working hours had to be spent in his master's service. The system of compulsory labor, known in France as the *corvée,* was in full force in Germany, and in some districts entailed no less than three days' work a week. The peasant was expected to keep the buildings on his lord's estate in good repair and to carry the produce of the estate to market; he drove his lord's carriage and carried his messages. Also he had to spend some years of his youth in his lord's household as a member of the domestic staff. However, it was possible for the serf to become a landowner, though his tenure was always hedged round with restrictions. He had to cultivate his land in a prescribed manner, under his lord's supervision, and could neither alienate nor mortgage it without permission. In some cases he was compelled to sell its produce, in others forbidden to sell it; in any case he was bound to keep the land under cultivation. Moreover, his children did not inherit his entire estate, some part of it being usually withheld by his lord.

It must not be thought that I am describing ancient or obsolete laws; these provisions can be found even in the code drawn up by Frederick the Great and put in force by his successor at the very time when the French Revolution was getting under way.

In France such conditions had long since passed away; the peasants could move about, buy and sell, work, and enter into contracts as they liked. Only in one or two eastern provinces, recent annexations, some last vestiges of serfdom lingered on; everywhere else it had wholly disappeared. Indeed, the abolition of serfdom had taken place in times so remote that its very date had been forgotten. However, as a result of recent research work it is now known that as early as the thirteenth century serfdom had ceased to exist in Normandy.

Meanwhile another revolution, of a different order, had done much to improve the status of the French peasant; he had not merely ceased to be a serf, he had also become a landowner. Though this change had far-reaching consequences, it is apt to be overlooked, and I propose to devote some pages to this all-important subject.

Until quite recently it was taken for granted that the splitting up of the landed estates in France was the work of the Revolution, and the Revolution alone; actually there is much evidence in support of the contrary view. Twenty years or more before the Revolution we find complaints being made that land was being subdivided to an unconscionable extent. "The practice of partitioning inheritances," said Turgot, writing at about this time, "has gone so far that a piece of land which just sufficed for a single family is now parceled out between five or six sons. The result is that the heirs and their families soon find that they cannot depend on the land for their livelihood and have to look elsewhere." And some years later Necker declared that there was "an inordinate number" of small country estates in France.

In a confidential report made to an Intendant shortly before the Revolution I find the following observations: "Inheritances are being subdivided nowadays to an alarming extent. Everybody insists on having his share of the land, with the result that estates are broken up into innumerable fragments, and this process of fragmentation is going on all the time." One might well imagine these words to have been written by one of our contemporaries.

I have been at great pains to make, as it were, a cadastral survey (i.e., of the distribution of land) of the old régime and have to some extent, I think, succeeded. Under the provisions of the law of 1790, which imposed a tax on land, each parish was required to draw up a return of all the privately owned land within its boundaries. Most of these documents are lost, but I have discovered some in certain villages and on comparing them with their modern equivalents have found that in these villages the number of landowners was as high as half, often two thirds, of the present number. These figures are impressive, and all the more so when we remember that the population of France has risen by over twenty-five per cent since that time.

Then, as in our own day, the peasant's desire for owning land was nothing short of an obsession and already all the passions to which possession of the soil gives rise in present-day France were active. "Land is always sold above its true value," a shrewd contemporary observer remarked, "and this is due to the Frenchman's inveterate craving to become a landowner. All the savings of the poorer classes, which in other countries are invested in private companies or the public funds, are used for buying land."

When Arthur Young visited France for the first time, among a multitude of new experiences, none impressed him more than the extent to which ownership of the soil was vested in innumerable peasant proprietors; half the cultivable land was owned by them. "I had no idea," he often says, "that such a state of affairs existed anywhere" — and in fact none such existed outside France.

There had once been many peasant proprietors in England, but by now their number had greatly dwindled. Everywhere in Germany and in all periods a limited number of free peasants had enjoyed full ownership of the land they worked. The special, often highly peculiar laws regulating the cultivator's ownership of land are set forth in the oldest German *Books of Customs,* but this type of ownership was always exceptional, there never were many of these small landed proprietors.

It was chiefly along the Rhine that at the close of the eighteenth century German farmers owned the land they worked and enjoyed almost as much freedom as the French small proprietor; and it was there, too, that the revolutionary zeal of the French found its earliest adepts and took most permanent effect. On the other hand, the parts of Germany which held out longest against the current of new ideas were those where the peasants did not as yet enjoy such privileges — and this is, to my mind, a highly suggestive fact.

Thus the prevalent idea that the breakup of the big estates in France began with the Revolution is erroneous; it had started long before. True, the revolutionary governments sold the estates owned by the clergy and many of those owned by the nobility; however, if we study the record of these sales (a rather tedious task, but one which I have on occasion found rewarding) we discover that most of the parcels of land were bought by people who already had land of their own. Thus, though estates changed hands, the number of landowners was increased much less than might have been expected. For, to employ the seemingly extravagant, but in this case correct, expression used by Necker, there were already "myriads" of such persons.

What the Revolution did was not to parcel out the soil of France, but to "liberate" it — for a while. Actually these small proprietors had much difficulty in making a living out of the land since it was subject to many imposts from which there was no escaping.

That these charges were heavy is undeniable, but, oddly enough, what made them seem so unbearable was something that, on the face of it, should have had the opposite effect: the fact that, as in no other part of Europe, our agriculturists had been emancipated from the control of their lords — a revolution no less momentous than that which had made them peasant proprietors.

At this point something must be said about those lucrative privileges which our forefathers usually had in mind when they spoke of "feudal rights," since it was these that most affected the life of the general public.

It is hard to say today which of these rights were still in force in 1789 and in what they consisted. There had been a vast number of them and by then many had died out or been modified almost out of recognition; indeed, the exact meaning of the terms in which they are described (about which even contemporaries were not very clear) is extremely hard to ascertain today. Nevertheless, my study of works by eighteenth-century experts on feudal law and my researches into local usages have made it clear to me that the rights still functioning in 1789 fell into a relatively small number of categories; others survived, no doubt, but they were operative only in exceptional cases.

Of the old seigneurial *corvée,* or statutory labor obligation, traces remained everywhere, but half obliterated. Most of the toll charges on the roads had been reduced or done away with, though there were few provinces in which some had not survived. Everywhere the resident seigneur levied dues on fairs and markets, and everywhere enjoyed exclusive rights of hunting. Usually he alone possessed dovecotes and pigeons, and it was the general rule that farmers must bring their wheat to their lord's mill and their grapes to his wine press. A universal and very onerous right was that named *lods et ventes;* that is to say an impost levied by the lord on transfers of land within his domain. And throughout the whole of France the land was subject to quitrents, ground rents, dues in money or in kind payable by the peasant proprietor to his lord and irredeemable by the former. Varied as they were, all these obligations had one common feature: they were associated with the soil or its produce, and all alike bore heavily on the cultivator.

The lords spiritual enjoyed similar privileges. For though the Church derived its authority from a different source and had aims and functions quite different from those of the temporal power, it had gradually become tied up with the feudal system and, though never fully integrated into it, was so deeply involved as to seem part and parcel of it.

Bishops, canons, and abbots owned fiefs or quitrents in virtue of their ecclesiastical status, and usually monasteries had seigneurial rights over the villages on whose land they stood. The monastery had serfs in the only part of France where serfdom had survived, employed forced labor, levied dues on fairs and markets, had the monopoly of the communal wine press, bakehouse, mill, and the stud bull. Moreover, the clergy enjoyed in France – as indeed in all Christian Europe – the right of levying tithes.

The point, however, on which I would lay stress is that exactly the same feudal rights were in force in every European land and that in most other countries of the continent they pressed far more heavily on the population than in France. Take, for example, the lord's right to forced labor, the *corvée.* It was rarely exercised and little oppressive in France, whereas in Germany it was stringent and everywhere enforced.

Moreover, when we turn to the feudal rights which so much outraged our fathers and which they regarded as opposed not merely to all ideas of justice but to the spirit of civilization itself (I am thinking of the tithe, irredeemable ground rents, perpetual charges, *lods et ventes,* and so forth, all that in the somewhat grandiloquent language of the eighteenth century was styled "the servitude of the land"), we find that all these practices obtained to some extent in England and, indeed, are still found there today. Yet they do not prevent English husbandry from being the best organized and most productive in the modern world; and, what is perhaps still more remarkable, the English nation seems hardly aware of their existence.

Why then did these selfsame feudal rights arouse such bitter hatred in the heart of the French people that it has persisted even after its object has long since ceased to exist? One of the reasons is that the French peasant had become a landowner, and another that he had been completely emancipated from the control of his lord. (No doubt there were other reasons, but these, I think, were the chief ones.)

If the peasant had not owned his land he would hardly have noticed many of the charges which the feudal system imposed on all real estate. What could the tithe matter to a man who had no land of his own? He could simply deduct it from the rent. And even restrictions hampering agriculture mean nothing to an agriculturist who is simply cultivating land for the benefit of someone else.

Moreover, if the French peasant had still been under his lord's control, the feudal rights would have seemed much less obnoxious, because he would have regarded them as basic to the constitution of his country.

When the nobles had real power as well as privileges, when they governed and administrated, their rights could be at once greater and less open to attack. In fact, the nobility was regarded in the age of feudalism much as the government is regarded by everyone today; its exactions were tolerated in view of the protection and security it provided. True, the nobles enjoyed invidious privileges and rights that weighed heavily on the commoner, but in return for this they kept order, administered justice, saw to the execution of the laws, came to the rescue of the oppressed, and watched over the interests of all. The more these functions passed out of the hands of the nobility, the more uncalled-for did their privileges appear — until at last their mere existence seemed a meaningless anachronism.

I would ask you to picture to yourself the French peasant as he was in the eighteenth century — or, rather, the peasant you know today, for he has not changed at all. His status is different, but not his personality. See how he appears in the records from which I have been quoting: a man so passionately devoted to the soil that he spends all his earnings on buying land, no matter what it costs. To acquire it he must begin by paying certain dues, not to the government but to other landowners of the neighborhood, who are as far removed as he from the central administration and almost as powerless as he. When at long last he has gained possession of this land which means so much to him, it is hardly an exaggeration to say that he sinks his heart in it along with the grain he sows. The possession of this little plot of earth, a tiny part, his very own, of the wide world, fills him with pride and a sense of independence. But now the neighbors aforesaid put in an appearance, drag him away from his cherished fields, and bid him work elsewhere without payment. When he tries to protect his seedlings from the animals they hunt, they tell him to take down his fences, and they lie in wait for him at river crossings to exact a toll. At the market there they are again, to make him pay for the right of selling the produce of his land, and when on his return home he wants to use the wheat he has put aside for his daily needs, he has to take it to their mill to have it ground, and then to have his bread baked in the lord's oven. Thus part of the income from his small domain goes to supporting these men in the form of charges which are imprescriptible and irredeemable. Whatever he sets out to do, he finds these tiresome neighbors barring his path, interfering in his simple pleasures and his work, and consuming the produce of his toil. And when he has done with them, other fine gentlemen dressed in black step in and take the greater part of his harvest. When we remember the special temperament of the French peasant proprietor in the eighteenth century, his ruling interests and passions, and the treatment accorded him, we can well understand the rankling grievances that burst into a flame in the French Revolution.

For even after it had ceased to be a political institution, the feudal system remained basic to the economic organization of France. In this restricted form it was far more hated than in the heyday of feudalism, and we are fully justified in saying that the very destruction of some of the institutions of the Middle Ages made those which survived seem all the more detestable. . . .

How, though the reign of Louis XVI was the most prosperous period of the monarchy, this very prosperity hastened the outbreak of the Revolution

There can be no question that the exhaustion of the kingdom under Louis XIV began at the very time when that monarch's arms were triumphant throughout Europe. Indeed, the first symptoms of an economic decline made their appearance in the years of his most spectacular successes; France was ruined long before she had ceased to be victorious. The gloomy picture of "administrative statistics" given by Vauban is familiar to all students of the period. In memoranda addressed to the Duke of Burgundy at the close of the seventeenth century, even before that ill-fated War of the Spanish Succession had begun, all the Intendants without exception drew attention to the progressive decline of our national prosperity; nor do they regard this as a new phenomenon. "In this district," one Intendant writes, "the population has been diminishing for a number of years"; another reports that "in this once rich and flourishing town all the old industries have died out"; a third that "there once were many factories in this province, all are derelict today"; a fourth that "our cultivators used to get much bigger crops from their land than they do now, indeed, agriculture was in a vastly better state twenty years ago." And an Intendant stationed at Orléans reported that both population and production had declined twenty per cent during the past thirty years. Any of my readers who are still enamored of absolutism and warlike monarchs would do well to peruse these records.

Since these calamities were chiefly due to defects inherent in the constitution, the death of Louis XIV and the coming of peace did nothing to restore prosperity. When discussing the administration and the social economy of France, all contemporary writers agree that there were no signs of recovery in the provinces, some going so far as to say that things were going from bad to worse. Paris alone, according to them, was growing more populous and wealthier. Intendants, ex-Ministers, and businessmen were at one, on this point, with our men of letters.

Personally I must confess I do not share the view that there was a continuous decline in the prosperity of France during the first half of the eighteenth century. Nonetheless, the fact that this opinion was so widespread and expressed by such well-informed observers proves that, anyhow, no visible progress was being made. From all the administrative records of the period that have come under my notice I gather that at this time the whole social system was the prey of a curious lethargy. The government did little more than keep to the beaten track of the old routine without ever striking out in new directions; municipal authorities did hardly anything to make living conditions in the towns healthier or more agreeable; even private enterprise was in the doldrums.

Some thirty or forty years before the Revolution, however, a change came over the scene. There were stirrings of a kind hitherto unknown throughout the social system, at first so faint as to be almost imperceptible, but steadily becoming more and more apparent. Year by year these movements spread, at an increasing tempo, until the whole nation seemed to be in the throes of a rebirth. But a rebirth in no literal sense, for what was coming to life was not the France of long ago, and the new spirit animating the nation made short work of all that it resuscitated. For the minds of men were in a ferment, every Frenchman was dissatisfied with his lot and quite decided to better it. And this rankling discontent made him at once impatient and fiercely hostile to the past; nothing would content him but a new world utterly different from the world around him.

Before long the government itself was infected by this spirit; to all appearances the administrative system remained as it had always been but within there was a change of heart. The laws were not altered but differently enforced.

I have already pointed out that the Controller-General and Intendants of 1740 were quite unlike the Controller-General and Intendants of 1780. Factual evidence of the difference can be found in the official correspondence of the two periods. True, the Intendant of 1780 had the same functions, the same subordinates, the same despotic power as his predecessor, but his aims were not the same. The Intendant of an earlier day busied himself chiefly with keeping his province well in hand, levying the militia, and, above all, collecting the *taille*. The 1780 Intendant had quite other interests; he was always trying to think up plans for increasing the wealth of his province. Roads, canals, industries, and commerce were his chief preoccupations, and that famous financial expert of the past, the Duc de Sully, was regarded by our executive officers as a paragon of wisdom.

It was in this period that the agricultural societies, of which I have already spoken, arose, organized competitions, and awarded prizes. Some of the Controller-General's publications read more like treatises on agriculture than official circulars. This change in the mentality of the central administration was most apparent in the new methods adopted for collecting taxes. The laws on the subject were as unjust, harsh, and arbitrary as ever, but they were now more leniently handled.

"When I began to study our fiscal legislation," writes Mollien in his *Memoirs,* "I was shocked by what I found there: fines, imprisonment, even corporal punishment could be inflicted by special courts for mere remissness on the taxpayer's part, while the local employees of the tax farmers, by means of their 'decisive oath,' could exercise tyrannical control over almost all estates and persons. Fortunately I did not confine myself to a mere perusal of the code, and I soon discovered that the same differences existed between its clauses and their application as between the methods of the old financiers and the new. The courts always tended to treat such offenses less seriously, and to impose light sentences."

In 1787 the Provincial Assembly of Lower Normandy, while deploring the malpractices of the fiscal authorities, went on to say: "We must admit, however, that during the last few years they have been showing much less harshness and a willingness to consider cases on their merits."

This is confirmed when we turn to the records of the period; they often evince a genuine respect for civic freedom and the rights of individuals. Particularly striking is a real concern for the hardships of the poor, which was far to seek in the earlier records. Rarely do we find the fiscal authorities harassing people who are not in a position to pay their taxes; remissions of taxation are more frequent, poor relief is more liberally granted. During this period the King increased the sums bespoken for the establishment of "charity workshops" in rural areas, and for the assistance of the poor, and time and again he sanctioned new grants of this order. I find that over 80,000 *livres* were distributed in poor relief in a single province, Upper Guienne, in 1779; 40,000 *livres* in Tours, in 1784; 48,000 in Normandy, in 1787. Louis XVI took a personal interest in these benefactions and did not leave them solely to the discretion of his Ministers. Thus when in 1776 an Order in Council fixed the compensation to be paid to certain peasants whose lands were in the neighborhood of royal game preserves and whose crops had suffered for this reason, the King drew up the preamble with his own hand. Turgot records that when handing him the document that kindly, ill-starred monarch said, "You see, I, too, do my share of work." If the old régime were depicted under its final aspect, the picture would, in fact, be flattering—but sadly far from the truth.

Parallel with these changes in the mentality of the rulers and the ruled there was an advance as rapid as it was unprecedented in the prosperity of the nation. This took the usual forms: an increase in the population and an even more spectacular increase in the wealth of individuals. The American war did not check this upward movement; though the State fell yet more heavily in debt, private persons went on making fortunes; also, they worked harder than in the past, showed more initiative and resourcefulness.

"Since 1774," wrote a member of the government, "the general expansion of industry has been bringing in more money by way of taxes on commodities." When we compare the contracts made at successive periods of the reign of Louis XVI between the State and the finance companies to which the taxes were farmed out by the Crown, we find that the sums paid by these companies shot up every year. The payments made by the tax farmers in 1786 exceeded those of 1780 by fourteen million *livres.* "We reckon that the revenue from taxes on commodities"—thus Necker in the 1781 budget—"rises by two millions yearly."

Arthur Young declared that in 1788 Bordeaux was a busier commercial center than Liverpool, and added that in recent times the progress of overseas commerce had been more rapid in France than even in England, and French trade had doubled in volume during the past twenty years.

A study of comparative statistics makes it clear that in none of the decades immediately following the Revolution did our national prosperity make such rapid forward strides as in the two preceding it. Only the thirty-seven years of constitutional monarchy, which were for us a time of peace and plenty, are in any way comparable in this respect with the reign of Louis XVI.

At first sight it seems hard to account for this steady increase in the wealth of the country despite the as yet unremedied shortcomings of the administration and the obstacles with which industry still had to contend. Indeed, many of our politicians, being unable to explain it, have followed the example of Molière's physician, who declared that no sick man could recover "against the rules of medicine" – and simply denied its existence. That France could prosper and grow rich, given the inequality of taxation, the vagaries of local laws, internal customs barriers, feudal rights, the trade corporations, the sales of offices, and all the rest, may well seem hardly credible. Yet the fact remains that the country did grow richer and living conditions improved throughout the land, and the reason was that though the machinery of government was ramshackle, ill regulated, inefficient, and though it tended to hinder rather than to further social progress, it had two redeeming features which sufficed to make it function and made for national prosperity. Firstly, though the government was no longer despotic, it still was powerful and capable of maintaining order everywhere; and secondly, the nation possessed an upper class that was the freest, most enlightened of the day and a social system under which every man could get rich if he set his mind to it and keep intact the wealth he had acquired.

The King still used the language of a master but in actual fact he always deferred to public opinion and was guided by it in his handling of day-to-day affairs. Indeed, he made a point of consulting it, feared it, and bowed to it invariably. Absolute according to the letter of the law, the monarchy was limited in practice. In 1784 Necker frankly recognized this as an accepted fact in an official declaration. "Few foreigners have any notion of the authority with which public opinion is invested in present-day France, and they have much difficulty in understanding the nature of this invisible power behind the throne. Yet it most certainly exists."

The belief that the greatness and power of a nation are products of its administrative machinery alone is, to say the least, shortsighted; however perfect that machinery, the driving force behind it is what counts. We have only to look at England, where the constitutional system is vastly more complicated, unwieldy, and erratic than that of France today. Yet is there any other European country whose national wealth is greater; where private ownership is more extensive, takes so many forms, and is so secure; where individual prosperity and a stable social system are so well allied? This is not due to the merits of any special laws but to the spirit animating the English constitution as a whole. That certain organs may be faulty matters little when the life force of the body politic has such vigor.

It is a singular fact that this steadily increasing prosperity, far from tranquilizing the population, everywhere promoted a spirit of unrest. The general public became more and more hostile to every ancient institution, more and more discontented; indeed, it was increasingly obvious that the nation was heading for a revolution.

Moreover, those parts of France in which the improvement in the standard of living was most pronounced were the chief centers of the revolutionary movement. Such records of the Ile-de-France region as have survived prove clearly that it was in the districts in the vicinity of Paris that the old order was soonest and most drastically superseded. In these parts the freedom and wealth of the peasants had long been better assured than in any other *pays d'élection*. Well before 1789 the system of forced labor (as applied to individuals) had disappeared in this region. The *taille* had become less onerous and was more equitably assessed than elsewhere. The Order in amendment of this tax must be studied if we wish to understand how much an Intendant of the time could do by way of improving—or worsening—the lot of an entire province. As set forth in this Order the impost in question assumes a very different aspect from that with which we are familiar. Tax commissioners were to be sent by the government yearly to each parish and all the inhabitants were to be summoned to appear before them. The value of all property subject to tax was to be assessed in public, the means of each taxpayer to be determined after hearing both parties, and finally, the incidence of the *taille* was to be fixed by the authorities in concert with all the taxpayers. The arbitrary powers of the Syndic and uncalled-for measures of coercion were abolished. No doubt the vices inherent in the whole system of the *taille* could not be eradicated; whatever improvements were made in the manner of collecting it, it affected only one class of taxpayers and was levied not only on their chattels but on the industries they carried on. Nevertheless, the *taille* as levied in the Ile-de-France was very different from the tax which still bore that name in nearby revenue subdivisions of the country.

Around the Loire estuary, in the Poitou fenlands, and the *landes* of Brittany the methods of the past were kept to more tenaciously than in any other part of France. Yet it was in these regions that civil war blazed up after the outbreak of the Revolution and the inhabitants put up the most passionate and stubborn resistance to it.

Thus it was precisely in those parts of France where there had been most improvement that popular discontent ran highest. This may seem illogical—but history is full of such paradoxes. For it is not always when things are going from bad to worse that revolutions break out. On the contrary, it oftener happens that when a people which has put up with an oppressive rule over a long period without protest suddenly finds the government relaxing its pressure, it takes up arms against it. Thus the social order overthrown by a revolution is almost always better than the one immediately preceding it, and experience teaches us that, generally speaking, the most perilous moment for a bad government is one when it seeks to mend its ways. Only consummate statecraft can enable a King to save his throne when after a long spell of oppressive rule he sets to improving the lot of his subjects. Patiently endured so long as it seemed beyond redress, a grievance comes to appear intolerable once the possibility of removing it crosses men's minds. For the mere fact that certain abuses have been remedied draws attention to the others and they now appear more galling; people may suffer less, but their sensibility is exacerbated. At the height of its power feudalism did not inspire so much hatred as it did on the eve of its eclipse. In the reign of Louis XVI the most trivial pinpricks of arbitrary power caused more resentment than the thoroughgoing despotism of Louis XIV. The brief imprisonment of Beaumarchais shocked Paris more than the *dragonnades* of 1685.

In 1780 there could no longer be any talk of France's being on the downgrade; on the contrary, it seemed that no limit could be set to her advance. And it was now that theories of the perfectibility of man and continuous progress came into fashion. Twenty years earlier there had been no hope for the future; in 1780 no anxiety was felt about it. Dazzled by the prospect of a felicity undreamed of hitherto and now within their grasp, people were blind to the very real improvement that had taken place and eager to precipitate events.

Aside from such considerations of a general order there were specific and no less potent reasons for this changed mentality. Though, like all other government departments, the financial administration had been thoroughly overhauled, it still had the vices inherent in all despotic systems, and since the Treasury accounts were never audited or published, some of the worst practices of the reigns of Louis XIV and Louis XV still prevailed. Moreover, the very efforts of the government to increase national prosperity, the reliefs and bounties it distributed, constantly imposed new burdens on the budget with which incoming revenue did not keep pace. Thus Louis XVI was involved in financial difficulties even worse than those of his predecessors. Like them he persistently kept his creditors waiting, like them he borrowed money right and left, without publicity and without stint, and his creditors were never sure of being paid the interest due on loans; indeed, even their capital was always at the mercy of the monarch's good will.

An eyewitness whom we have every reason to trust, since he was better placed than any other to see what was going on, tells us that "the French of those days were exposed to constant risks in their dealings with their own government. If they invested capital in government securities they could never feel certain that the interest would be forthcoming on the due dates; if they built ships, repaired roads, or supplied clothing to the army they had no guaranty for the sums disbursed and were reduced to assessing the risks involved in taking up a government contract as one calculates them for some highly speculative venture. During this period," he adds with much good sense, "when owing to the rapid progress of industry a larger number of people than ever before had acquired the possessive instinct and a taste for easy living, those who had entrusted the State with a portion of their capital were all the more irritated by the frequent breaches of contract committed by a debtor who, more than any other, should have made a point of keeping faith."

There was nothing new in these delinquencies on the part of the administration; what was new was the indignation they aroused. The vices of the financial system had been far more glaring in the past, but a great change had supervened in both the methods of government and in the structure of society, a change which made the French far more acutely conscious of these vices than they had been hitherto.

During the last twenty years the government had become more energetic, had launched out into a host of activities to which until then it had never given a thought, and as a result had become the greatest consumer of industrial products and the chief employer of labor in the kingdom. The number of persons having monetary dealings with it, subscribing to its loans, living on wages paid by it, and speculating in government-sponsored enterprises had enormously increased. Never before had the interests and fortunes of private individuals been so closely bound up with those of the State. Thus the mismanagement of the State finances, which formerly had affected only the administration, now brought ruin to many homes. In 1789 the State owed nearly six hundred million *livres* to its creditors, who themselves were for the most part deep in debt and made common cause with all who likewise were being victimized by the remissness of the government in punctually fulfilling its obligations. As the number of malcontents increased, they became ever more loudspoken in their protests; for the habit of speculation, the passion for money-making, and the taste for comfortable living that had developed along with the expansion of commerce and industry made such grievances seem intolerable to those very persons who, thirty years earlier, would have endured them without a murmur.

Thus it was that *rentiers,* merchants, manufacturers, businessmen, and financiers — the section of the community usually most averse to violent political changes, warm supporters of the existing government, whatever it may be, and essentially law-abiding even when they despise or dislike the laws — now proved to be the most strenuous and determined advocates of reform. What they demanded most vociferously was nothing short of a radical change in the entire financial administration of the country, and they failed to realize that a change so revolutionary would spell the downfall of the constitution as a whole. It is hard to see how a catastrophe could have been averted. On the one hand was a nation in which the love of wealth and luxury was daily spreading; on the other a government that while constantly fomenting this new passion, at the same time frustrated it — and by this fatal inconsistency was sealing its own doom.

THE PEOPLE

HIPPOLYTE ADOLPHE TAINE

Hippolyte Adolphe Taine, born a generation later than Michelet and Tocqueville, was not an historian by profession. He was already renowned as a critic of both French and English literature when in 1871 he began work on his history of contemporary France which was to be his primary concern up to the time of his death in 1893. Based on new and wide-ranging research in the archives, the critical view of the Old Regime and the Revolution which it presented was buttressed by an impressive array of detailed documentary evidence. The excerpt that follows is taken from the first volume, published in 1875.

I

EXAMINE administrative correspondence for the last thirty years preceding the Revolution. Countless statements reveal excessive suffering, even when not terminating in fury. Life to a man of the lower class, to an artisan, or workman, subsisting on the labor of his own hands, is evidently precarious; he obtains simply enough to keep him from starvation and he does not always get that. Here, in four districts, "the inhabitants live only on buckwheat," and for five years, the apple crop having failed, they drink only water. There, in a country of vineyards, "the vine-dressers each year are reduced, for the most part, to begging their bread during the dull season." Elsewhere, several of the day-laborers and mechanics, obliged to sell their effects and household goods, die of the cold; insufficient and unhealthy food generates sickness, while in two districts, thirty-five thousand persons are stated to be living on alms. In a remote canton the peasants cut the grain still green and dry it in the oven, because they are too hungry to wait. The intendant of Poitiers writes that "as soon as the workhouses open, a prodigious number of the poor rush to them, in spite of the reduction of wages and of the restrictions imposed on them in behalf of the most needy." The intendant of Bourges notices that a great many *métayers* have sold off their furniture and that "entire families pass two days without eating," and that in many parishes the famished stay in bed most of the day because they suffer less. The intendant of Orléans reports that "in Sologne, poor widows have burned up their wooden bedsteads and others have consumed their fruit trees" to preserve themselves from the cold, and he adds, "nothing is exaggerated in this statement; the cries of want cannot be expressed; the misery of the rural districts must be seen with one's own eyes to obtain an idea of it." From Rioni, from La Rochelle, from Limoges, from Lyons, from Montauban, from Caen, from Alençon, from Flanders, from Moulins come similar statements by other intendants. One might call it the interruptions and repetitions of a funeral knell; even in years not disastrous it is heard on all sides. In Burgundy, near Chatillon-sur-Seine, "taxes, seigniorial dues, the tithes, and the expenses

From *The Ancient Régime,* translated by John Durand from H. A. Taine, *L'Ancien Régime* (Paris, 1875), Book Fifth, Chapter I, pp. 335–348. Henry Holt and Company.

of cultivation, divide up the productions of the soil into thirds, leaving nothing for the unfortunate cultivators, who would have abandoned their fields, had not two Swiss manufacturers of calicoes settled there and distributed about the country forty thousand francs a year in cash." In Auvergne, the country is depopulated daily; many of the villages have lost, since the beginning of the century, more than one-third of their inhabitants. "Had not steps been promptly taken to lighten the burden of a downtrodden people," says the provincial assembly in 1787, "Auvergne would have forever lost its population and its cultivation." In Comminges, at the outbreak of the Revolution, certain communities threaten to abandon their possessions, should they obtain no relief. "It is a well-known fact," says the assembly of Haute-Guyenne, in 1784, "that the lot of the most severely taxed communities is so rigorous as to have led their proprietors frequently to abandon their property. Who is not aware of the inhabitants of Saint-Servin having abandoned their possessions ten times and of their threats to resort again to this painful proceeding in their recourse to the administration? Only a few years ago an abandonment of the community of Boisse took place through the combined action of the inhabitants, the seignior and the *decimateur* of the community"; and the desertion would be still greater if the law did not forbid persons liable to the *taille* abandoning overtaxed property, except by renouncing whatever they possessed in the community. In the Soissonais, according to the report of the provincial assembly, "misery is excessive." In Gascony the spectacle is "heart-rending." In the environs of Toule, the cultivator, after paying his taxes, tithes and other dues, remains empty-handed. "Agriculture is an occupation of steady anxiety and privation, in which thousands of men are obliged to painfully vegetate." In a village in Normandy, "nearly all the inhabitants, not excepting the farmers and proprietors, eat barley bread and drink water, living like the most wretched of men, so as to provide for the payment of taxes with which they are overburdened." In the same province, at Forges, "many poor creatures eat oat bread, and others bread of soaked bran, this nourishment causing many deaths among infants." People evidently live from day to day; whenever the crop proves poor they lack bread. Let a frost come, a hailstorm, an inundation, and an entire province is incapable of supporting itself until the coming year; in many places even an ordinary winter suffices to bring on distress. On all sides hands are seen outstretched to the king, who is the universal almoner. The people may be said to resemble a man attempting to wade through a pool with the water up to his chin, and who, losing his footing at the slightest depression, sinks down and drowns. Existent charity and the fresh spirit of humanity vainly strive to rescue them; the water has risen too high. It must subside to a lower level and the pool be drawn off through some adequate outlet. Thus far the poor man catches breath only at intervals, running the risk of drowning at every moment.

II

Between 1750 and 1760, the idlers who eat suppers begin to regard with compassion and alarm the laborers who go without dinners. Why are the latter so impoverished, and by what mischance, on a soil as rich as that of France, do those lack bread who grow the grain? In the first place many farms remain uncultivated, and, what is worse, many are deserted. According to the best observers "one-quarter of the soil is absolutely lying waste; . . . Hundreds and hundreds of *arpents* of heath and moor form extensive deserts." "Let a person traverse Anjou, Maine, Brittany, Poitou, Limousin, la Marche, Berry, Nivernais, Bourbonnais and Auvergne, and he finds one-half of these provinces in heaths, forming immense plains all of which might be cultivated." In Touraine, in Poitou and in Berry they form solitary expanses of thirty thousand *arpents*. In one canton alone, near Preuilly, forty thousand *arpents* of good soil consist of heath. The agricultural society of Rennes declares that two-thirds of Brittany is lying waste. This is not sterility but decadence. The régime invented by Louis XIV has produced its effect; the soil for a century past is reverting back to a wild state. "We see only abandoned and ruinous chateaux; the principal towns of the fiefs, in which the nobility formerly lived at their ease, are all now occupied by poor *métayer* herdsmen whose scanty labor hardly suffices for their subsistence and a remnant of tax ready to disappear through the ruin of the proprietors and the desertion of the settlers." In the election-district of Confolens a piece of property rented for 2,956 *livres* in 1665, brings in only 900 *livres* in 1747. On the confines of la Marche and of Berry a domain which, in 1660, honorably supported two seigniorial families is now simply a small unproductive *métayer*-farm; "the traces of the furrows once made by the ploughshare being still visible on the surrounding heaths." Sologne, once flourishing, becomes a marsh and a forest; a hundred years earlier it produced three times the quantity of grain; two-thirds of its mills are gone; not a vestige of its vineyards remains; "grapes have given way to the heath." Thus abandoned by the spade and the plough, a vast portion of the soil ceases to feed man, while the rest, poorly cultivated, scarcely provides the simplest necessities.

In the first place, on the failure of a crop, this portion remains untilled; its occupant is too poor to purchase seed; the intendant is often obliged to distribute seed, without which the disaster of the current year would be followed by sterility the following year. Every calamity, accordingly, in these days affects the future as well as the present; during the two years of 1784 and 1785, around Toulouse, the drought having caused the loss of all draft animals, many of the cultivators are obliged to let their fields lie fallow. In the second place, cultivation, when it does take place, is carried on according to mediaeval modes. Arthur Young in 1789, considers that French agriculture has not progressed beyond that of the tenth century. Except in Flanders and on the plains of Alsace, the fields lie fallow one year out of three and oftentimes one year out of two. The implements are poor; there are no ploughs made of iron; in many places the plough of Virgil's time is still in use. Cart-axles and wheel-tires are made of wood, while a harrow often consists of the trestle of a cart. There are few animals and but little manure; the capital bestowed on cultivation is three times less than that of the present day. The yield is slight; "our ordinary farms," says a good observer, "taking one with another return about six times the seed sown." In 1778, on the rich soil around Toulouse, wheat returns about five for one, while at the present day it yields eight to one and more. Arthur Young estimates that, in his day, the English acre produces twenty-eight bushels of grain, and the French acre eighteen bushels, and that the value of the total product of the same area for a given length of time is thirty-six pounds sterling in England and only twenty-five in France. As the parish roads are frightful, and transportation often impracticable, it is clear that, in remote cantons, where poor soil yields scarcely three times the seed sown, food is not always obtainable. How do they manage to live until the next crop? This is the question always under consideration previous to, and during, the Revolution. I find, in manuscript correspondence, the syndics and mayors of villages estimating the quantities for local subsistence at so many bushels in the granaries, so many sheaves in the barns, so many mouths to be filled, so many days to wait until the August wheat comes in, and concluding on short supplies for two, three and four months. Such a state of inter-communication, and of agriculture condemns a country to periodical famines, and I venture to state that, alongside of the small-pox which, out of eight deaths, causes one, another endemic disease exists, as prevalent and as destructive, and this disease is starvation.

We can easily imagine the people as sufferers by it, and, especially, the peasant. An advance in the price of bread prevents him from getting any, and even without that advance, he obtains it with difficulty. Wheat bread costs, as at the present day, three *sous* per pound, but as the average day's work brought only nineteen *sous* instead of forty, the day-laborer, working the same time, could buy only the half of a loaf instead of a full loaf. Taking everything into account, and wages being estimated according to the price of grain, we find that the husbandman's manual labor then procured him 959 *litres* of wheat, while nowadays it gives him 1,851 *litres;* his well-being, accordingly, has advanced ninety-three per cent; which suffices to show to what extent his predecessors suffered privations. And these privations are peculiar to France. Through analogous observations and estimates Arthur Young shows that in France those who lived on field labor, and they constituted the great majority, are seventy-six per cent less comfortable than the same laborers in England, while they are seventy-six per cent less well in health. The result is that, in seven-eighths of the kingdom, there are no farmers but simply *métayers*. The peasant is too poor to undertake cultivation on his own account, possessing no agricultural capital. "The proprietor, desirous of improving his land, finds no one to cultivate it but miserable creatures possessing only a pair of hands; he is obliged to advance everything for its cultivation at his own expense, animals, implements and seed, and even to advance the wherewithal to this *métayer* to feed him until the first crop comes in." "At Vatan, for example, in Berry, the *métayers,* almost every year, borrow bread of the proprietor in order to await the harvesting." "Very rarely is one found who is not indebted to his master at least one hundred *livres* a year." Frequently the latter proposes to abandon the entire crop to them on condition that they demand nothing of him during the year; "these miserable creatures" have refused; left to themselves, they would not be sure of keeping themselves alive. In Limousin and in Angoumois their poverty is so great "that, deducting the taxes to which they are subject, they have no more than from twenty-five to thirty *livres* each person per annum to spend; and not in money, it must be stated, but counting whatever they consume in kind out of the crops they produce. Frequently they have less, and when they cannot possibly make a living the master is obliged to support them. . . . The *métayer* is always reduced to just what is absolutely necessary to keep him from starving." As to the small proprietor, the villager who ploughs his land himself, his condition is but little better. "Agriculture, as our peasants practise it, is a veritable drudgery; they die by thousands in childhood, and in maturity they seek places everywhere but where they should be." In 1783, throughout the plain of the Toulousain they eat only maize, a mixture of flour, common seeds and very little wheat; those on the mountains feed, a part of the year, on chestnuts; the potato is hardly known, and, according to Arthur Young, ninety-nine out of a hundred peasants would refuse to eat it. According to the reports of intendants, the basis of food, in Normandy, is oats; in the election-district of Troyes, buckwheat; in the Marche and in Limousin, buckwheat with chestnuts and radishes; in Auvergne, buckwheat, chestnuts, milk-curds and a little salted goat's meat; in Beauce, a mixture of barley and rye; in Berry, a mixture of barley and oats. There is no wheat bread; the peasant consumes inferior flour only because he is unable to pay two *sous* a pound for his bread. There is no butcher's meat; at best he kills one pig a year. His dwelling is built of clay (*pise*), roofed with thatch, without windows, and the floor is the beaten ground. Even when the soil furnishes good building materials, stone, slate and tile, the windows have no sashes. In a parish in Normandy, in 1789, "most of the dwellings consist of four posts." They are often mere stables or barns "to which a chimney has been added made of four poles and some mud." Their clothes are rags, and often, in winter these are muslin rags. In Quercy and elsewhere, they have no stockings, or shoes or *sabots* (wooden shoes). "It is not in the power of an English imagination," says Arthur Young, "to figure the animals that waited on us here at the *Chapeau Rouge*. Some things that called themselves by courtesy Souillac women, but in reality walking dung-hills. But a neatly dressed, clean waiting-girl at an inn, will be looked for in vain in France." On reading descriptions made on the spot we see in France a similar aspect of country and of peasantry as in Ireland, at least in its broad outlines.

III

In the most fertile regions, for instance, in Limagne, both cottages and faces denote "misery and privation." "The peasants are generally feeble, emaciated and of slight stature." Nearly all derive wheat and wine from their homesteads, but they are forced to sell this to pay their rents and imposts; they eat black bread, made of rye and barley, and their sole beverage is water poured on the lees and the husks. "An Englishman who has not travelled can not imagine the figure made by infinitely the greater part of the countrywomen in France." Arthur Young, who stops to talk with one of these in Champagne, says that "this woman, at no great distance, might have been taken for sixty or seventy, her figure was so bent and her face so hardened and furrowed by labor, but she said she was only twenty-eight." This woman, her husband and her household, afford a sufficiently accurate example of the condition of the small proprietary husbandmen. Their property consists simply of a patch of ground, with a cow and a poor little horse; their seven children consume the whole of the cow's milk. They owe to one seignior a *franchard* (forty-two pounds) of flour, and three chickens; to another three *franchards* of oats, one chicken and one *sou*, to which must be added the *taille* and other imposts. "God keep us!" she said, "for the *tailles* and the dues crush us." What must it be in districts where the soil is poor! "From Ormes (near Chatellerault), as far as Poitiers," writes a lady, "there is a good deal of ground which brings in nothing, and from Poitiers to my residence (in Limousin) twenty-five thousand *arpents* of ground consist wholly of heath and sea-grass. The peasantry live on rye, of which they do not remove the bran, and which is as black and heavy as lead. In Poitou, and here, they plough up only the skin of the ground with a miserable little plough without wheels.... From Poitiers to Montmorillon it is nine leagues, equal to sixteen of Paris, and I assure you that I have seen but four men on the road and, between Montmorillon and my own house, which is four leagues, but three; and then only at a distance, not having met one on the road. You need not be surprised at this in such a country. . . . Marriage takes place as early as with the grand seigniors," doubtless for fear of the militia. "But the population of the country is no greater because almost every infant dies. Mothers having scarcely any milk, their infants eat the bread of which I spoke, the stomach of a girl of four years being as big as that of a pregnant woman. . . . Their rye crop this year was ruined by the frost on Easter day; flour is scarce; of the twelve *métairies* owned by my mother, four of them may, perhaps, have some on hand. There has been no rain since Easter; no hay, no pasture, no vegetables, no fruit. You see the lot of the poor peasant. There is no manure, and there are no cattle. . . . My mother, whose granaries used to be always full, has not a grain of wheat in them, because, for two years past, she has fed all her *métayers* and the poor."

"The peasant is assisted," says a seignior of the same province, "protected, and rarely maltreated, but he is looked upon with disdain. If kindly and pliable he is made subservient, but if ill-disposed he becomes soured and irritable. . . . He is kept in misery, in a abject state, by men who are not at all inhuman but whose prejudices, especially among the nobles, lead them to regard him as of a different species of being. . . . The proprietor gets all he can out of him; in any event, looking upon him and his oxen as domestic animals, he puts them into harness and employs them in all weathers for every kind of journey, and for every species of carting and transport. On the other hand, this *métayer* thinks of living with as little labor as possible, converting as much ground as he can into pasturage, for the reason that the product arising from the increase of stock costs him no labor. The little ploughing he does is for the purpose of raising low-priced provisions suitable for his own nourishment, such as buckwheat, radishes, etc. His enjoyment consists only of his own idleness and sluggishness, hoping for a good chestnut year and doing nothing voluntarily but procreate"; unable to hire farming hands he begets children. The rest, ordinary laborers, have small supplies, "living on the spontaneous, and on a few goats which devour everything." Often again, these, by order of Parlement, are killed by the keepers. A woman, with two children in swaddling clothes, having no milk, "and without an inch of ground," whose two goats, her sole resource, had thus been slain, and another, with one goat slain in the same way, and who begs along with her boy, present themselves at the gate of the chateau; one receives twelve *livres,* while the other is admitted as a domestic, and henceforth, "this village is all bows and smiling faces." In short, they are not accustomed to benefactions; the lot of all these poor people is to endure. "As with rain and hail, they regard as inevitable the necessity of being oppressed by the strongest, the richest, the most skillful, the most in repute," and this stamps on them, "if one may be allowed to say so, an air of painful suffering."

In Auvergne, a feudal country, covered with extensive ecclesiastic and seignioral domains, the misery is the same. At Clermont-Ferrand, "there are many streets that can for blackness, dirt and scents only be represented by narrow channels cut in a night dunghill." In the inns of the largest bourgs, "closeness, misery, dirtiness and darkness." That of Pradelles is "one of the worst in France." That of Aubenas, says Young, "would be a purgatory for one of my pigs." The senses, in short, are paralyzed. The primitive man is content so long as he can sleep and get something to eat. He gets something to eat, but what kind of food? To put up with the indigestible mess a peasant here requires a still tougher stomach than in Limousin; in certain villages where, ten years later, every year twenty or twenty-five hogs are to be slaughtered, they now slaughter but three. On contemplating this temperament, rude and intact since Vercingetorix, and, moreover, rendered more savage by suffering, one cannot avoid being somewhat alarmed. The Marquis de Mirabeau describes "the votive festival of Mont-Dore, savages descending from the mountain in torrents, the curate with stole and surplice, the justice in his wig, the police corps with sabres drawn, all guarding the open square before letting the bagpipers play; the dance interrupted in a quarter of an hour by a fight; the hootings and cries of children, of the feeble and other spectators, urging them on as the rabble urge on so many fighting dogs; frightful-looking men, or rather wild beasts covered with coats of coarse wool, wearing wide leather belts pierced with copper nails, gigantic in stature, which is increased by high *sabots,* and making themselves still taller by standing on tiptoe to see the battle, stamping with their feet as it progresses and rubbing each other's flanks with their elbows, their faces haggard, and covered with long matted hair, the upper portion pallid, and the lower distended, indicative of cruel delight and a sort of ferocious impatience. And these folks pay the *taille!* And now they want to take away their salt! And they know nothing of those they despoil, of those whom they think they govern, believing that, by a few strokes of a cowardly and careless pen, they may starve them with impunity up to the final catastrophe! Poor Jean-Jacques, I said to myself, had any one despatched you, with your system, to copy music amongst these folks he would have had some sharp replies to make to your discourses!" Prophetic warning and admirable foresight in one whom an excess of evil does not blind to the evil of the remedy! Enlightened by his feudal and rural instincts, the old man at once judges both the government and the philosophers, the Ancient Régime and the Revolution.

IV

Misery begets bitterness in a man; but ownership coupled with misery renders him still more bitter. He may have submitted to indigence but not to spoilation – which is the situation of the peasant in 1789, for, during the eighteenth century, he had become the possessor of land. But how could he maintain himself in such destitution? The fact is almost incredible, but it is nevertheless true. We can only explain it by the character of the French peasant, by his sobriety, his tenacity, his rigor with himself, his dissimulation, his hereditary passion for property and especially for that of the soil. He had lived on privations, and economized *sou* after *sou*. Every year a few pieces of silver are added to his little store of crowns buried in the most secret recess of his cellar; Rousseau's peasant, concealing his wine and bread in a pit, assuredly had a yet more secret hiding-place; a little money in a woolen stocking or in a jug escapes, more readily than elsewhere, the search of the clerks. Dressed in rags, going barefoot, eating nothing but coarse black bread, but cherishing the little treasure in his breast on which he builds so many hopes, he watches for the opportunity which never fails to come. "In spite of privileges," writes a gentleman in 1775, "the nobles are daily being ruined and reduced, the Third-Estate making all the fortunes." A number of domains, through forced or voluntary sales, thus pass into the hands of financiers, of men of the quill, of merchants, and of the well-to-do bourgeois. Before undergoing this total dispossession, however, the seignior, involved in debt, is evidently resigned to partial alienations of his property. The peasant who has bribed the steward is on hand with his hoard. "It is poor property, my lord, and it costs you more than you get from it." This may refer to an isolated patch, one end of a field or meadow, sometimes a farm whose farmer pays nothing, and generally worked by a *métayer* whose wants and indolence make him an annual expense to his master. The latter may say to himself that the alienated parcel is not lost since, some day or other, through his right of repurchase, he may take it back, while in the meantime, he enjoys a *cens*, drawbacks, and the lord's dues. Moreover, there is on his domain and around him, extensive open spaces which the decline of cultivation and depopulation have left a desert. To restore the value of this he must surrender its proprietorship. There is no other way by which to attach man permanently to the soil. And the government helps him along in this matter. Obtaining no revenue from the abandoned soil, it assents to a provisional withdrawal of its too weighty hand. By the edict of 1766, a piece of cleared waste land remains free of the *taille* for fifteen years, and, thereupon, in twenty-eight provinces four hundred thousand *arpents* are cleared in three years.

This is the mode by which the seignioral domain gradually crumbles away and decreases. Towards the last, in many places, with the exception of the chateau and the small adjoining farm, which brings in two or three thousand francs a year, nothing is left to the seignior but his feudal dues; the rest of the soil belongs to the peasantry. Forbonnais already remarks, towards 1750, that many of the nobles and of the ennobled "reduced to extreme poverty but with titles to immense possessions," have sold off portions to small cultivators at low prices, and often for the amount of the *taille*. Towards 1760, one-quarter of the soil is said to have already passed into the hands of agriculturists. In 1772, in relation to the *vingtième*, which is levied on the net revenue of real property, the intendant of Caen, having completed the statement of his quota, estimates that out of one hundred and fifty thousand "there are perhaps fifty thousand whose liabilities did not exceed five *sous* and perhaps still as many more not exceeding twenty *sous*." Contemporary observers authenticate this passion of the peasant for real property. "The savings of the lower classes, which elsewhere are invested with individuals and in the public funds, are wholly destined in France to the purchase of land." "Accordingly the number of small rural holdings is always on the increase. Necker says that there is an *immensity* of them." Arthur Young, in 1789, is astonished at their great number and "inclines to think that they form one-third of the kingdom." That would already be about the proportion, and the proportion would still be the same, were we to compare the number of proprietors with the number of inhabitants.

The small cultivator, however, in becoming a possessor of the soil assumes its charges. Simply as day-laborer, and with his arms alone, he was only partially affected by the taxes; "where there is nothing the king loses his dues." But now, vainly is he poor and declaring himself still poorer; the fisc has a hold on him and on every portion of his new possessions. The collectors, peasants like himself, and jealous, by virtue of being his neighbors, know how much his property, exposed to view, brings in; hence they take all they can lay their hands on. Vainly has he labored with renewed energy; his hands remain as empty, and, at the end of the year, he discovers that his field has produced him nothing. The more he acquires and produces the more burdensome do the taxes become. In 1715, the *taille* and the poll-tax, which he alone pays, or nearly alone, amounts to sixty-six millions of *livres;* the amount is ninety-three millions in 1759 and one hundred and ten millions in 1789. In 1757, the imposts amount to 283,156,000 *livres;* in 1789 to 476,294,000 *livres.*

Theoretically, through humanity and through good sense, there is, doubtless, a desire to relieve the peasant and pity is felt for him. But, in practice, through necessity and routine, he is treated according to Cardinal Richelieu's precept, as a beast of burden to which oats are measured out for fear that he may become too strong and kick, "a mule which, accustomed to his load, is spoiled by more long repose than by work."

SEIGNEURIAL OBLIGATIONS DURING THE REIGN OF LOUIS XVI

ALPHONSE AULARD

Alphonse Aulard was the first professional historian to devote his full time and energies to the French Revolution. He was the first appointee to the chair of Revolutionary history established at the University of Paris in 1885, and he spent the remainder of his life lecturing and writing on that subject. He also edited and published some of its most important official documents. Although he concentrated primarily on its political aspects, he occasionally, as in the following excerpt, turned his attention to social and economic questions. He was a staunch defender of the Revolution and its republican ideals against the attacks of Taine from the right and Mathiez from the left. The selection which follows is taken from the course of lectures which he gave at the Sorbonne in the winter of 1912–1913.

TO DETERMINE the reasons which the Convention had for abolishing all seigneurial rights, I have been led to examine the question of whether feudal obligations were increased and whether they in fact became more intolerable during the reign of Louis XVI, before the night of August 4, as certain well-informed writers have given us to understand. . . .

I must confess immediately that I have not succeeded in establishing the basis for a sure reply to that question and it does not seem to me that a clear yes or no answer can be given to it, however far we may push our research and whatever information we may ultimately be able to turn up. Perhaps one may at some time be able to say yes or no to the extent of affirming that in certain instances and in certain regions feudal obligations became, or appeared to become, heavier and that in other instances and other regions they appear to have become less so.

We should point out first that the words *feudalism, feudal regime, feudal rights* were not used in 1789 in their rigorously historical sense, and what they actually referred to was the condition so aptly called "civil feudalism" by Tocqueville, which had succeeded to the political feudalism of an earlier era. In his report of September 4, 1789 to the Committee on Feudalism, Merlin (of Douai) said, "There can be no question about the object of our efforts. There is to be no limit to our research into and examination of feudal rights; and you know, gentlemen, that although the words *feudal rights,* when defined in rigorous fashion, designate only those rights which are derived from a feudal contract of which sub-infeudation is the essential principle, it is nevertheless customary to extend its meaning to cover all the rights which are ordinarily found in the hands of seigneurs and which make up in their totality what Dumoulin has called the *feudal complex.*

From Alphonse Aulard, *Etudes et leçons sur la révolution française* (7e Série, Paris, 1913), Lecture I, pp. 2–4, 19–30, 32–44. Translated by the Editor. By permission Presses Universitaires de France.

And so although seigneurial rents, rights of *champart, corvées, banalités,* and other payments symbolic of former servitude etc. are not strictly speaking feudal rights, we will concern ourselves with them and I would even go so far as to say that to allow ourselves to be diverted from such consideration would be to misinterpret the intentions of the decree of the National Assembly which established our Committee."

Thus within this *feudal complex* an attempt was made to distinguish between obligations relating to a person and more or less implying a kind of personal servitude, and "real" obligations which applied to things such as property and inheritances.

There is no question but that personal obligations became less burdensome during the reign of Louis XVI being specifically lightened . . . as a result of the edict of August 1779 by which he abolished serfdom on his royal domaine. . . .

And so a part of the feudal burden, a small part but one especially difficult to bear, was lifted from the shoulders of some. Accordingly, over all, the feudal burden was less heavy in 1789, on the eve of the Revolution, than in 1778.

With respect to the other elements of the feudal burden, that is to say, the "real" obligations, one could perhaps say with respect to the one which constituted the seigneurial right *par excellence,* the one in which was seen the most obvious symbol of feudal lordship, the *cens,* or quit-rent, that it was relatively less heavy than in former times by virtue of the fact that it remained at the same rate.[1] But without going into the complicated question of the purchasing power of money in different periods, there is no doubt that 10 *sols* in 1595 or in 1640 were worth more than in 1785 or 1789. It was less strain therefore for the tenant to pay his quit-rent under Louis XVI than it had been for his ancestor in the 16th and 17th centuries. It seems then that here again the feudal burden had lost a little of its weight.

Too little, some will say: A few *sols,* is it worth even speaking of them? Yes, it is worth it because these few *sols* when added to the many other *sols* or *livres* which the peasant had to pay added to his burden. He surely felt, being so poor, the weight of even this small payment. But there was added on top of that, in the case of a purchase or sale, a much weightier obligation to pay to the seigneur called *lods et ventes* which varied according to the custom of the area from 10 to 12 or 15 per cent of the purchase price of the land.

If *lods et ventes* were paid in cash, the *cens* itself, by which I mean the annual payment, was made sometimes partly in cash and partly in kind, or only in kind, as, for example, so many bushels of wheat, or sometimes in the form of *champart* [*champart* was a payment in kind of a fixed proportion of the harvest] instead of a *cens* which had all the annoyance and odium which that form of payment always provoked. In the case of payments in kind, time had not lightened the burden, but had made it heavier since the products of the soil were worth more in money. There was more than one *cahier* in which a protest was made against paying the *cens* in kind.

To know whether, over all, and in all its forms the *cens* was really less heavy and just how much less heavy at the time of Louis XVI as compared to Louis XIV, for example, it would be necessary to determine from all the *terriers* [legal documents on which the peasants' obligations were recorded] an exact accounting of the payments in kind and the payments in money, an accounting of the amount of the *lods et ventes,* as well as the allowances accorded to the tenants on the rate of *lods et ventes.* In brief it would require statistics which we are lacking for the very good reason that a very great number of the land registers were destroyed by the insurrections or the laws of the Revolutionary period.

There can then be no certainty that the

[1] The payments made to cover the *cens* could, in principle, be neither increased nor decreased. A piece of property which payed 10 *sols* in 1595 or in 1640 had to pay 10 *sols* in 1785 or 1789, neither more nor less; that was the law and the rule.

weight of the *cens* had become less heavy at the end of the Old Regime; but perhaps one can say that it can be presumed to have done so.

Was there a lightening of the burden in the sense that the seigneurs were less rigorous in demanding the payment of seigneurial dues, the obligations which were owed them?

We have the papers relating to the administration of the lands of a few seigneurs. There are, for example, . . . some relating to the financial affairs of L-H-T de Cossé-Brissac, Duke de Cossé. . . . We have most of the registers of the correspondence which the chief-agent of the duke carried on with the nine agents of his lands. . . . It can be seen that this grand seigneur was a philanthropist who gave the most humane instructions to his chief-agent to follow with respect to his tenants. Thus in the case of *lods et ventes,* the duke agreed in very many cases to the remission of a third, or where custom would not allow that, of a quarter. To collect the seigneurial dues, *cens, champart* or others, the agents were to resort to the law as little as possible. . . .

There were then, on the eve of the Revolution, some great seigneurs who were not hard on their tenants, who collected their feudal dues with moderation and who were compassionate to the poor and miserable. The philosophy of the century, put in practice, inspired these individual acts of generosity which were not rare.

These are the facts and the hypotheses which enable us to say that feudalism had become less burdensome during the reign of Louis XVI. M. Sagnac who . . . tried to show that, on the contrary, it had become more burdensome, pointed out that even after the customary payments were recorded and the rights of the seigneurs thus limited by being recorded in black and white, there were some attempts on the part of the king and the seigneurs to extend these rights either by the resumption of former ones which had fallen in abeyance, or by outright usurpation. . . .

[It is true that] under Louis XVI a royal order issued on July 28, 1786 specified that payments of *lods et ventes* should be made to the king by the holders of islands and filled lands. The king and the princes of the blood took over more and more swamps and uncultivated lands. Some seigneurs made more and more use of certain rights . . . which allowed them to take back a third of the common lands alleged to have been conceded by them to the village in earlier times. The exercise of the *banalités,* so disagreeable to the peasants, seems to have been aggravated here and there.

What we are sure of, however, is that if during the reign of Louis XVI the peasants complained very much more than formerly about their feudal obligations, it was because these obligations appeared to them to be less bearable than in former times.

By the criticisms which the *philosophes* had made of these obligations; by the success of the little pamphlet of Boncerf on the evil-effects of feudal obligations (1776), a success which the Parlement of Paris had made all the more resounding by condemning it; by the propaganda of a humanitarian and egalitarian philosophy; by the very proposals and liberal attitudes of the seigneurs; by the conversation of educated bourgeoisie and also many of the clergy with the peasants; by all these means the idea was spread across the countryside that these obligations were unjust. Since well-informed men in whom the peasants had confidence had told them that things ought to be changed, the peasants found the feudal burden heavier than heretofore.

Some may make objection to the contention that the peasants were really less poor than formerly, by pointing to the fact that they bought land and that many of them had become landowners. Unquestionably the fact that peasant holdings, as has been said, continued to increase in the second half of the 18th century no longer seems doubtful. M. Loutchisky has shown that on the eve of the Revolution in Limousin, in 85 parishes in the district of Tulle, out of 247,000 *arpents* of land, the peasants owned 137,000 and in 43 parishes in the district of Brire, out of 63,000 *arpents* the peasants owned 34,000, or more than half of the total. On the other hand in these two districts he found only 17 per cent of the peasants who were not owners. There are even some villages where property is less divided today than it was under the Old Regime. But do these purchases denote any easier living conditions for the peasant?

Yes and no. Yes, in the sense that if these purchases became more frequent, it seems logical to conclude that the peasants had more money than formerly and that the regime had thus become less heavy. No, if one admits that certain economic and social conditions had led the nobility to sell their land and thus a great many opportunities to become a landowner had simultaneously been offered to the peasantry at the end of the 18th century which had not been offered to them in earlier times.

In truth, it was by unbelievable frugality and economy that the peasants succeeded in acquiring so many parcels of land. It must be said that they spent almost nothing or practically nothing for their nourishment, being satisfied, in the Limousin area, for example, with coarse bread, soup, some chestnuts, beans (potatoes were not in general use) a little salt pork occasionally and a little wine at times. They spent little for their dress, being content with that crude, stiff and durable cloth called drugget which lasted for several generations, and also with linen no less coarse. Almost all the little hard cash which they managed to hide from the royal tax collector or the seigneurial agents they secreted in a wool sock from which it was withdrawn only to purchase land in very small bits, purchases amounting sometimes to only one hundred *livres*, or even fifty, or sometimes even less.

Even with land life was no easier for the peasant buyer. In more than one instance he found himself half ruined by the strain of the acquisition and obliged to leave his land and go to the city to work as a mason in order to bring back money enough to complete the payment for his acquisition, or in some instances to also pay for the heavy burden of the *lods et ventes*.

When these payments were completed, did his property, by the increased income it paid him, serve to make him less poor and more happy? No. The feudal burden which when he was a share-cropper, renter, day laborer, or domestic weighed only partly on his shoulders, now weighed entirely on them since he was now a landowner. The *cens* always, *champart* sometimes, the *banalités* always, the ecclesiastical *dîme* always, the disastrous effects of the seigneur's hunting rights; all these vexations of the feudal regime fell on the new owner and he felt more unfortunate than he had been before he had owned anything.

Thus the increase in peasant property ownership, far from mitigating the feudal regime, made it felt by more individuals and so to speak made the hatred of it more general on the eve of the Revolution.

Very many of the land registers (*terriers*) of the seigneurs were revised during the reign of Louis XVI and especially between the years 1780 and 1789. The old registers, in view of the changes and sub-divisions in the lands, had become in part unusable. The seigneurs no longer felt themselves to possess sufficiently clear titles at a time when the legitimacy of seigneurial rights was being contested by so many writers and when there was a whole movement of opinion against these rights, and when the Parlement of Paris was urging the seigneurs to resist the movement by asserting their prerogatives as proprietors. This is doubtless why the renewal of these land registers was then so general, or at least very frequent. MM. Champion and Sagnac are right to say that this was one of the facts which made the seigneurial regime appear more disagreeable, more heavy.

A *terrier* or a *terrier* book, or a *terrier* paper may be described as a "register containing an enumeration of the individuals who fell within the jurisdiction of a seigneurie and of the details of the rights, *cens* and rents which were due to it."

The drawing up or renewal of these

registers was onerous to the landholders on whom it imposed the payment of certain fees. The lord, therefore, could not do it whenever he wished. He could do it only every thirty years in the area under the jurisdiction of the Parlement of Paris, and, in Auvergne, Bourbonnais, Lyonnais, Forez, Beaujolais, Maçonnais he could do it only every twenty years. . . . The permission of the king was necessary each time and he had, for this reason to obtain an official letter from the crown in order to constrain those owing payments and obligations by virtue of their holding property on his manor, to come before a notary commissioned by him for the purpose, to make formal recognition of these payments and other obligations in proper form.

There arose in 1786 a situation in connection with the fees to be paid by the landholders on a seigneurie which stirred up numerous and lively complaints which are found expressed in many *cahiers*. I mean the issuance of royal letters concerning the amount of the fees to be paid to the attorney drawing up the land register. . . . The king said that with respect to declarations by holders of bourgeois lands in the towns, the fee should be 30 *sous* for the first article and 15 for the ones thereafter; for rural lands it should be 15 *sous* and 7½ *sous*. . . .

The Parlement of Paris had issued regulations on this point in 1739 and 1744 which had fixed the fees at 5 *sous* for the first article and 2½ *sous* for the others. The increase of the above over these rates appeared enormous to the tenants who lived in the jurisdiction of the Parlement of Paris, and even, as is seen by the *cahiers*, to holders living in other regions. . . . According to M. Sagnac, on the basis of the *cahiers* and especially on that of the parish of Cerans (Sarthe), there were some seigneurs who did not give any remuneration to their commissioner or lawyer revising their register. Others let them have half of a year's income from any new obligations which they could turn up, or in other cases, half of the arrears found owing which had been overlooked or had not been required up until that time.

M. Sagnac is right. That happened. To the witnesses of it which he produces I can add another very reliable one in Quercy. . . . And these abuses are to be found in other regions besides Quercy. But one must not attribute them everywhere to the cupidity of the lawyers, who, receiving no set honorarium from the seigneurs, had to recoup from the tenants. It seems that it was rather the rule for the seigneurs to pay their commissioners for renewing their land registers.

All these commissioners were not then starving men without salaries, reduced to living by sucking the blood of the poor.

Doubtless, even if disinterested personally in the outcome, it is probable that they often took the side of the seigneur against the tenant and they intimidated more than one peasant to get him to accept the declaration of his obligations which they proposed without daring to contest it. However, there was a legal limit to these excesses and injustices. If the tenant refused to make the declaration demanded, the seigneur had to take him before a royal court and not before seigneurial judges as was the case with the payment of the *cens* and certain other obligations. There is little question, however, but what the renewal of the *terriers* increased the revenues of certain seigneurs. M. Sagnac cites some texts which seem to prove it. . . . In some cases the tenants used to paying little, were very unhappy and complained that they were being asked for more than they owed, when in reality they were perhaps being asked only for what they really owed and nothing more.

These complaints are numerous in the *cahiers* but those doing the complaining cite very few precise or specific facts. Even when it was Dupont de Nemours who was writing we are disappointed. The following appears in the *cahier* of the bailliage of Nemours: "And what can one say of the fees which for centuries or many years have not been collected and which the seigneurs cause to be revived solely by the authority of their collection agent, without the justice of the king having pronounced in the matter? There are some in this bailliage which were just begun to be collected in this manner eight years ago." The smallest specific instance would have aided our investigation.

Even in the complaints received by the Committee on Feudal Rights, in 1790 at a time when people were less timid there are only much too vague assertions. Thus on August 10, 1789, Seguin, a priest of Sauveterre . . . wrote "I know a piece of land where the last renewals increased the rent by a sixth; I have verified it by the old leases and have warned the seigneur in vain." What piece of land? What seigneur? Abbé Seguin does not say. Is it even certain that seigneurial rights were involved since it was a question not of *terriers* or declarations but of rents and leases?

The same is true in connection with the ecclesiastical tithe. When the *cahiers* complain that it had been increased, they do not prove it or only make a very weak case.

One of the most frequent complaints in the *cahiers* or the addresses received by the Committee on Feudal Rights, was that the seigneurs had increased the size of the measures used for measuring the grain owed by the tenants either for all or part of the *cens,* or for *champart,* or for the tithe. That was asserted in 1791 by the municipal officials of Blanzac and other towns of the Charente region but without producing any proofs to support their contention.

. . . It is evident that there is no certainty as to the degree of the increase in the burden of feudal obligations under Louis XVI, if indeed it was increased at all. What is certain is that complaints were made sincerely, vigorously, and unanimously and that men felt that they suffered more from the feudal regime under Louis XVI than under Louis XV. Perhaps it was actually no heavier, but the peasant was simply less resigned to it.

As we have said, the enlightened views of the *philosophes* . . . had so strongly intensified the hatred of that which remained of the feudal regime that even the peasants began to be more aware of the iniquity of feudal rights.

THE BREAKDOWN OF THE ANCIEN RÉGIME

ALBERT MATHIEZ

Preeminent as the foremost Marxist interpreter of the Revolution, Albert Mathiez concentrated his scholarly talents on the illumination of its social and economic history. Although never a slavish follower of Marxian theory, he did, nevertheless, hold consistently to the view that the Revolution was primarily the work of the energetic and economically powerful bourgeois class. With typical Marxist antipathy to that class he questioned the high-mindedness and universality of its ideals and actions at all points. The following selection is a very brief excerpt from his one-volume history of the Revolution, and it is one of the few instances where he discusses conditions under the Old Regime.

OVER against the privileged classes and "officers" who were in possession of the State, new forces were gradually arising: those of trade and industry. On the one hand stood feudal and real property, on the other the personal wealth of the middle classes.

In spite of the fetters imposed by the system of *corporations* — though this was less oppressive than has been supposed — in spite of the internal duties and tolls (*péages*), in spite of the diversity of weights and measures, trade and industry had increased for a whole century past. The foreign trade of France was second only to that of England. Colonial produce was the monopoly of the mother country. Her possession of Santo Domingo alone provided her with one-half of the sugar consumed in the world. Her silk industry, which employed sixty-five thousand workmen at Lyons, was unrivalled. Her brandies, wines, stuffs, fashions, and furniture were sold in all parts of Europe. Even the metal industries, the development of which had been but recent, were progressing. Le Creusot, then known as Montcenis, was already a model workshop, equipped with the latest improvements, and Dietrich, the king of ironmasters at the time, employed hundreds of workmen in his blast-furnaces and forges in Lower Alsace, fitted out in the English style. In 1791 Bonaffé, a Bordeaux shipowner, had a fleet of thirty ships and a fortune of sixteen million *livres*. Nor was this millionaire an exception. Far from it. There were very great fortunes at Lyons, Marseilles, Nantes, Havre, and Rouen.

Economic development was so intense that the number of banks increased greatly under Louis XVI. The Caisse d'Escompte (Bank of Discount) of Paris already issued notes similar to those of the modern bank of France. Capital began to come together and form joint-stock companies: the India Company (*Compagnie des Indes*), fire- and life-insurance companies, the Paris water-supply company. The metal works of Montcenis were turned into a joint-stock company. The shares, quoted on the

Bourse alongside of the *rentes sur l'Hôtel de Ville,*[1] gave rise to active speculation. Dealings in futures were already a usual practice.

In 1789 the service of the public debt absorbed three hundred million *livres* a year; that is to say, more than half the total revenue of the State. The Company of the Farmers-General, which collected on behalf of the Crown the proceeds of the indirect taxes, *aides,*[2] *gabelle* (salt-tax), tobacco-duty, stamp-duties, had at its head financiers of the first rank, who vied in magnificence with the most splendid nobles. A great stir of business was making itself felt among the middle classes. The price of a place on the Stock Exchange doubled within a single year. Necker writes that France possessed nearly half the available cash in Europe. Merchants were buying the estates of noblemen with debts, and building fine mansions decorated by the best artists. Farmers-general had their *folies* (pleasure-houses) in the suburbs of Paris, like the great lords. The towns were being rebuilt and beautified.

An infallible sign that the wealth of the country was increasing was that the population was growing rapidly and the prices of commodities, land, and houses were steadily rising. France already contained twenty-five million inhabitants, twice as many as England or Prussia. Comfort was gradually spreading downwards, from the upper to the lower middle class and that of artisans and small shopkeepers. People dressed better and had better food than in former days. Above all, education was spreading. The daughters of commoners, who were now called "demoiselle" if they wore dresses with panniers, were buying pianos. The increased revenue from taxes on food-stuffs was evidence of the progress in comfort.

And so the Revolution was not to break out in an exhausted country but, on the contrary, in a flourishing land on a rising tide of progress. Poverty may sometimes lead to riots, but it cannot bring about great social upheavals. These always arise from a disturbance of the balance between the classes.

The middle classes certainly possessed the greater part of the fortune of France. They were advancing steadily, whereas the privileged orders were ruining themselves. Their very rise made them more acutely sensitive to the inferior legal status to which they were still condemned. Barnave became a revolutionary the day that his mother was turned out of the box which she was occupying in the theatre at Grenoble by a nobleman. Mme Roland complains that when she was asked to stay to dinner at the Château of Fontenay with her mother, it was served to them in the servants' quarters. How many enemies of the old régime were made by wounded self-esteem!

. . . The Revolution could come only from above. The working-classes, whose narrow horizon embraced nothing beyond their calling, were incapable of initiating it, still less of taking the control into their own hands. Industry on a large scale was in its first beginnings. Nowhere did the workmen form coherent groups. Those who were on the books of the *corporations,* and subordinate to them, were split up into rival workmen's associations (*compagnonnages*), more interested in petty squabbling than in presenting a united front to their employers. They hoped, moreover, to become employers in their turn and had a chance of doing so, since craftsmanship on a small scale was still the normal form of industrial production. As for the rest, those who were beginning to be employed in the "manufactories," many of them were peasants who regarded what they earned in industrial employment as a supplement to their agricultural earnings. Most of them were docile and respectful to the employers who provided them with work, so much so that in 1789 they looked upon them as their natural representatives. It is true that the workmen complained of their modest wages, which, to quote the testimony of Roland when he

[1] Loans issued by the State and secured upon the revenues of the City of Paris.

[2] This word had come to be used of taxes on consumption, especially upon liquor, snuff, etc.

was a factory-inspector, had not increased at the same rate as the price of commodities. There was sometimes agitation among them, but they did not as yet feel themselves to be a distinct class of the third estate.

The peasants were the beasts of burden of this society. Tithes, rents in money and in kind, forced labour, royal taxes, service in the militia, all these burdens fell upon them. Their lords' pigeons and game ravaged their crops with impunity. They lived in houses of mud, often covered with thatch, and sometimes with no chimneys. They tasted meat only on feast-days, and sugar only in case of illness. Compared with our peasants of today, they were wretched; and yet they were less miserable than their fathers had been, or than the peasants of Italy, Spain, Germany, Ireland, or Poland at the same period. By dint of toil and saving, some of them had succeeded in buying a piece of a field or pasturage. The rise in the value of agricultural produce had favoured the beginnings of emancipation. Those who had not succeeded in acquiring a little land were the most to be pitied. They were angry at having to share the common lands with their lords, at the abolition of the rights of common pasture and gleaning, which deprived them of the few resources which they had enjoyed under the system of primitive communism. There were also a number of day-labourers, who were often out of work, and were obliged to go from farm to farm in search of employment. It is hard to draw the line between them and the numerous class of vagabonds and beggars. It was from their ranks that was recruited the army of smugglers and dealers in contraband salt (*faux-sauniers*) who were perpetually at war with the excisemen (*gabelous*).

The workmen and peasants were capable of a brief movement of revolt when the yoke became too heavy, but could not see their way towards changing the social order. They were only just beginning to learn to read. But they had among them the priest and the local lawyer (*praticien*) to enlighten them: the priest, to whom they confided their sorrows, and the lawyer, who defended their interests in the courts. But the priests had read the literature of the day; they knew the scandalous existence led by their superiors in their sumptuous palaces, while they themselves subsisted meagrely on their pittance; and instead of preaching resignation to their flock, as in the past, they infected their minds with a little of the indignation and bitterness with which they were themselves filled. The country lawyer, for his part, obliged as he was by the exigencies of his profession to search among the old feudal deeds could not fail to arrive at a just estimate of the archaic titles which formed the basis of wealth and oppression. It was in the exercise of his profession of feudal expert that Babeuf learnt his contempt for property. He pitied the peasants from whom the greed of their lord – who employed him to set his muniments in order – set to work to extort fresh dues which had become obsolete.

Thus criticism was working underground which long preceded and prepared for the explosion. The opportunity had only to arise, and all this accumulated and stifled rage would lend force to the attacks of these poor wretches, stirred up and directed by a host of malcontents.

THE VILLAGE—WEALTH AND POVERTY OF THE RURAL CLASSES

FRANTZ FUNCK-BRENTANO

A Frenchman in spite of the Teutonic sound of his name, Frantz Funck-Brentano had a long and distinguished career as an historian and archivist in Paris at the beginning of this century. Known best as a medieval scholar and as an explorer of the byways of history such as the alleged poison plots which add lurid interest to the reign of Louis XIV, he approaches the Old Regime from the viewpoint of a medievalist. Perhaps this accounts in large measure for the obvious sympathy for this era which is evident in the following selection.

THE PEASANT

In France of old the country districts were of far more importance than the towns, especially towards the middle of the eighteenth century, at which period we see industry attaining a brilliant scope; here too we may say that under the Ancien Régime the family, of which we have already treated, and the village, which we are about to deal with, formed the foundations of the whole of society.

The celebrated picture of the tiller of the soil sketched by La Bruyère is well known:

> We see certain wild animals, male and female, spread over the country, dark, livid and tanned by the sun, clinging to the soil which they dig and turn up with invincible perseverance; they have some sort of articulate speech, and when they rise to their feet they display human faces, and are, in fact, men. They retire by night into their dens where they live on black bread, water and roots; they spare others the trouble of sowing, ploughing and gathering their daily bread, and in this way do not deserve to be lacking in what they have sown.

Perhaps nothing in our literature is more celebrated than this steel etching *à la Callot,* the quintessence of the history taught in French schools. Elsewhere La Bruyère says, "In towns one is brought up in utter indifference to things rural and of the fields." Doubtless he wished to give us a personal example.

The above lines of La Bruyère are only literature, written by a good writer for the sake of effect, which he attains. We might make of them one panel of a diptych, the second of which might be the following picture given by Sébastien Mercier:

> A rustic wedding at which the couple are seen proceeding to the church with their fingers lovingly intertwined and glancing at each other with looks expressing their simple feelings; the parents are following behind to that same altar where they themselves were married; the groomsmen in their Sunday clothes, with ribbons in their hats and flowers in their button-holes; the girls in white bodices looking with more assurance at their sweethearts on that special day; and the violin, somewhat squeaky it is true, gaily closing up the procession. . . .

Then comes the wedding feast:

From *The Old Regime in France* translated by Herbert Wilson from Frantz Funck-Brentano, *L'Ancien Régime* (1929), Chapter VIII, pp. 259–270, 282–285. By permission of Edward Arnold Ltd., London.

The village banquet, with its unaffected laughter, the table on the grass, the joy of the relatives, the wine pitcher ever replenished, the calf cut up and roasted whole. Next, the sprightly dances and lively frolics; the old white-haired folk wiping from their eyes their affectionate tears, the bridegroom, petulant and watching impatiently for the evening star to gleam forth, and on the morrow the bride somewhat pale, confused and happy, wondering and triumphant. . . .

Greuze, where are thy brushes?

But let us leave La Bruyère and Sébastien Mercier to reconcile their differences, and let us talk seriously.

Among the writers on the Ancien Régime there is one possessing a unique value in connection with country life. Retif de la Bretonne, the Burgundian peasant, who followed the plough up to the age of twenty, and lived in close relations with the people in his village, has described with robust pen the life led by his own people. In a large number of his books, particularly *La Vie de mon Père*—a masterpiece; in *Monsieur Nicolas,* an autobiography; *l'Ecole des pères,* and the *Paysan perverti,* we find descriptions of exceptional value, owing to their reality, relish and sincerity, of the village people and peasants of Burgundy in the first half of the eighteenth century.

Speaking of the two villages of Sacy (Dept. of the Yonne, *canton* of Vermenton) and Nitry (*canton* of Noyers), Retif writes:

"The inhabitants owned their land almost entirely; each one cultivated his share, and possessed cattle proportioned in number to the quantity of forage raised and the amount of manure he required."

VILLAGE ASSEMBLIES

In addition to privately owned property each village (they called them communities) possessed *communes* (common lands) belonging to all. But let us leave the description to our peasant:

"As the small parish of Sacy," says Retif, "possessed *communes,* it was governed like one family." The following words are of special interest and should be remembered. "Everything in it was decided by a plurality of votes at meetings which were held in the public square on Sundays and *fête* days, to which they were summoned by the ringing of the great bell. At these meetings were appointed the syndics, collectors of the *taille,* the watchmen to guard sown land and the vines, and the public herdsmen." On a former page we discussed these village assemblies in connection with the jurisdiction of the seigneur. The syndics were the officials of the rural communities and had nothing to do with the municipal administration.

The seigneur's representative presided at these meetings; the taxing officer (*Procureur Fiscal*) laid the matters to be discussed before the meeting, but each individual had the right to denounce any abuses he knew of, or to propose any measures that he considered to be useful. These matters were discussed then and there, and if they were of any consequence they would send the syndics to the Intendant's subdelegates to have them authorized. Further, at these meetings they would designate each year the section of the common woods to be cut by each member; this was drawn by lot, with the exception of the Curé, the chief (seigneur), when he was living there, and the two syndics to whom were assigned by name the best sections.

As we can see, this was rural self-government in all its integrity. We should particularly note that this picture of a village meeting given by Retif agrees in all its details with that presented at a later date by Cardinal Mathieu in the case of Lorraine, as the result of his study of the local archives.

Albert Babeau writes: "Forty thousand natural associations deliberated about their own interests and chose their own agents."

But let us look at the picture drawn by Cardinal Mathieu of the village assemblies in Lorraine:

The syndic was elected every year. The inhabitants assembled on a Sunday after Vespers either in front of the church, under the shade of the huge tree which had sheltered their rustic deliberations, sometimes for centuries past, or on the market-place; or may be in the seigneur's audience chamber, when there was one. There they would discuss among themselves almost the same matters as our own municipal councils do, and a few other questions besides. They would appoint the assessors and collectors, would agree upon the tithes which had been presented by the tithe collector for payment, fix the date for beginning the harvest, the wages of the herdsman and the schoolmaster; would decide upon what repairs were needed for the belfry tower, the Curé's house, the bridge over the stream, and the road leading to the next village. They would settle the sharing, sale or letting of the common lands, the manner of fulfilling the obligation of the *corvée;* would delegate the mayor (representing the seigneur) or the syndic (acting for the community) to go to the office of the Intendant, to the magistrate's court, or the person in authority, to ask permission, may be, to remove a cow or horse impounded by the watchman of a neighbouring village; lastly, they would listen to the statement of dues to be paid. Often the meetings became heated. . . . It sometimes happened that they would decide to bring an action against the seigneur, the Curé, or against a neighbouring community. . . .

It was not in reality a deliberative assembly, but a sort of public meeting of which the village notary kept the minutes.

Similar meetings of mothers were held on a Sunday after Vespers, to choose the official village midwife, and the Curé would preside. Possibly he may not have had sufficient acquaintance with the subject, and so there were sometimes complaints of the routine methods of the midwives chosen, some of whom were imbued with the quaintest superstitions.

It is clear that such a communal administration, comprising all the inhabitants of a village, would no longer be possible today, not only on account of the extent of many of our villages, but principally because of the multiplicity and complicated nature of the questions with which such assemblies would have to concern themselves. The autonomy of the different families forming the communities of earlier days, each one of which administered its own affairs like a small State, rendered the questions to be discussed very simple and few. There were some villages in which the only expenditure in common was for the upkeep of the clock in the belfry of the church. It was the schoolmaster's duty, as a rule, to wind up the weights.

As regards the election of the dignitaries and officials of the communities, this took place under the most ordinary circumstances in the world — amid the canvassing and intrigue which generally flourished in this kind of operation; they would elect the syndic, the schoolmaster, the tithe collector, the collector of the *taille,* the herdsman or common shepherd, the *va-de-pied,* that is, the rural postman, and the carrier whose duty it was to place the locality in communication with the neighbourhood.

We can readily imagine the confusion and disorder which could find their way into these meetings, especially in the eighteenth century with its changing customs and the lessening of the traditional respect for the head of the family, whose authority up till then had been the preponderating influence at the assemblies. Turgot complains of the uproar and commotion into which these meetings under the old elm had degenerated. Compelled to extend the field of their deliberations, the peasants no longer possessed the requisite knowledge, and groped about in the dark. Busybodies gave ready tongue to their grievances and the community lost its way in a host of law-suits, for in the course of the eighteenth century our peasants became madly litigious. It sometimes happened that Parliament quashed their decisions, but the Intendants constituted themselves their defenders.

The seigneur's voice was listened to no longer, nor that of his agent. In many localities the sale of the domain had brought a new family to the manor house; it was no longer the same family with which for centuries the parish had held close relations.

How many parishes which willingly had followed the counsels of their old seigneurial family came into conflict at the very outset with the one which had taken its place! The seigneur now lived at Court, and his domain was administered by a steward, and his land by a farmer. Seigneur and vassal no longer took any interest in each other. Towards the close of the Ancien Régime many parishes had reached the point of delegating their powers to various forms of municipal councils, as we do at the present day. The collector of the *taille* and the syndic had slipped more and more under the authority of the Intendant, or his subdelegate; in many villages the syndic had even become the King's agent in proportion as the seigneur, whether from absence or indifference, had become more or less a stranger to his "subjects," for it should be noted that the importance and independence of these village assemblies went on diminishing during the course of the eighteenth century, in proportion as the importance of the part played by the seigneur among his tenants grew feebler.

RUSTIC INTERIORS

The Seigneur of Nitry was a Knight of Malta. On the death of Maître Boujat, the judge of the seigneurial domain, who for the space of forty years had carried out his functions to the satisfaction of those in his jurisdiction, Retif's father was called upon to succeed him at the request of a deputation to the seigneur from the village. Retif speaks in terms of the greatest praise of the Curés of the two parishes of Nitry and Sacy. Messire Antoine Foudriat, the Curé of Nitry, "assisted the poor to pay the *taille*." Marriages were celebrated at four o'clock in the morning, a custom which was widespread.

Retif introduces us inside the homes of these worthy folk; we can see the heavy curtains with their woven patterns surrounding the beds, and the earthenware plates leaning against the dresser.

Several families would unite "to make up a three-horsed plough." Nicholas Retif had gone to a distance from Nitry with a comrade, and when passing through the village of Puits-de-Bon (Dept. of Yonne, *commune* of Noyers-en-Serein), he and his young friend knocked at a door. There they found some worthy peasants supping on a dish of salt pork, after which appeared black puddings. A great jug of wine was warming in front of the fire—they drank it hot. "The party was made up of three families regaling themselves together after sowing their crops. They were *'suitiers,'* that is, associated together to make up a three-horsed plough."

Let us now enter Retif de la Bretonne's own home:

> In the evening at supper, the only meal at which all the family could assemble together, Edmond Retif (the father) looked like a patriarch at the head of a numerous household, for, as a rule, there were twenty-two at table, including the ploughman, and the vine dressers (who in winter became threshers), the cowman, the shepherd, and two female servants, one of whom worked with the threshers, and the other looked after the cows and the dairy. All the company were seated at one table, the head of the family at the end, near the fire, with his wife by his side within reach of the dishes to be served—for she alone had the care of the kitchen. The female servants, who had been working all day, were sitting eating peacefully; then came the children of the family, seated in order of age, which was all that settled their places; next, the ploughman of longest service and his mates; then the vine dressers, after them the cowman, and the shepherd; the two women servants closed up the ranks. . . .

It was supper time, and as we said above, it was the only meal uniting the whole family together, and in the "family," following a good old custom, were comprised the women servants and labourers; during the daytime, their different occupations did not, in fact, allow of everybody meeting together at the same hour.

After supper the head of the family would read a few pages of Holy Scripture, accompanied with explanations and kindly remarks. This was followed by a short prayer, said in common, and then the last part of the catechism was recited by the little children. "After that all went to bed silently, for after evening prayers," said Retif, "laughter and loud conversation were forbidden."

In winter, when the evenings were longer, after the recitation of the catechism the head of the family would tell stories and old legends of the countryside, and give them the latest news, and then everyone was free to speak, and there would be laughter and joking. During Advent, Christmas carols were sung. We are far from La Bruyère's "wild animals," as one can see.

A mother sends his scanty wardrobe to her son who had left the village to go to the town:

"Edmond, I am sending you thick floss stockings and breeches of *fort-en-diable*,[1] two vests and your homespun coat for you to make a brave show on Sundays and *fête* days."

And how easy it is to understand this old peasant making his son, who wanted to become a bourgeois in the town, return to his native village:

"They would like to settle you in the town, would they! Tell me, my future posterity, what would become of you in a few years when lost among the population of the towns? Let us remain here, where everything is full of us, where everything reminds us of our honourable position! . . ."

We have another picture of village conditions and habits sketched by Marmontel. He too, like Retif, was a son of peasants, worthy people among whom he passed his early days. Marmontel is more literary than Retif, and his style is polished. His aim is to present us, not only with accurate pictures, but rounded and well-balanced sentences. Marmontel's pages do not possess the same zest, intense life, and high relief of the Burgundian's portraits, but the similarity between the two is none the less useful. They wrote at the same period, and while Retif introduces us to Burgundy, Marmontel takes us to the Limousin district.

Marmontel first saw the light of day and passed his early boyhood at Bort (Dept. of Corrèze) a little rustic village. In addition to the father and mother there lived under the same roof the two grandmothers, three aunts, and a "swarm of children." "Bort on the Dordogne was a place where any inequality in condition or fortune was scarcely felt. A little property, or some small form of industry and commerce made up the condition of nearly all the inhabitants. . . . Everyone was free, and usefully occupied."

He makes the following interesting remark: "The marriages they made were no anxiety to the family; there was so little inequality in their condition or fortune that the fathers and mothers were in agreement almost as soon as their children, and rarely did marriage end in a lessening of mutual love. . . ."

Marmontel had a little friend whose fair hair was always carefully combed, his clothes were clean and simple, and his linen always white. His name was Durand, and his father was a labourer in a neighbouring village. Marmontel was always delighted to go there. "How the good old man welcomed us! What fine cream, rich milk and good brown bread!"

The little fellow was spoilt by his grandmother. "She used to show me, like so many treasures, the provision she had made for the winter, her bacon, hams, sausages, pots of honey and jars of oil, her store of buckwheat, rye, peas and beans, her pile of radishes and chestnuts, her straw beds covered with fruit."

Marmontel continues:

The sheep-folds of Saint-Thomas clothed the women and children with their wool; my aunts spun the wool, as well as the hemp which provided us with linen; and in the evenings, by the light of a lamp burning oil made from our own walnuts, the young people near by would come and help us beat this good hemp, making an enchanting picture.

[1] *Fort-en-diable:* a familiar term, denoting a special material of very strong texture. (H. W.)

The harvest of the little farm provided our subsistence; the wax and honey from the bees, which one of my aunts cultivated with care, gave a return with little expense; the oil pressed out from our walnuts when still fresh, had a savour and odour which we preferred to the taste and smell of olive oil. The flat buckwheat cakes, buttered when hot with that excellent butter of Mont d'Or, were a great treat for us. I do not know anything we enjoyed more than our radishes and chestnuts, and on winter evenings when these fine radishes were roasting round the fire, or when we heard the water boiling in the saucepan wherein were cooking those savoury tender chestnuts, our hearts would palpitate with joy. . . .

Consequently in a household where everything was made use of, these little things combined made up the comforts of life in a small way, and not much expense was entailed in providing for all our necessities. There was dead wood in abundance in the forests near by which was of little value, and my father was allowed to take what he wanted. The excellent mountain butter and most delicious cheeses were local and cost little; wine was not dear, and my father drank it sparingly. . . .

Christmas! And the Christmas feast! "How the same delight came round every year!" writes Marmontel. "We looked forward to it, but took care to conceal our expectations. While we were at Mass the soup of green cabbage, the black puddings, the sausages, the dish of rosy salt pork, the cakes, apple-fritters fried in lard, were all mysteriously made ready by her (the grandmother) and one of her sisters. . . . After Mass all these wonderful things were found on the table, and we would shout with cries of delight. . . ."

Here again it is a far cry to La Bruyère's "wild animals."

Retif has drawn in many places portraits of these heads of peasant families, called in Lorraine *"chefs de feux"*; in the Midi *"caps d'hostal* (chefs d'hôtel, chefs de maison)," and in other localities *"ménagers."* Ch. de Ribbe states that "the *ménager* has been for centuries one of the corner stones of the edifice of local liberties." Henri de Sourdis, when sent by Richelieu on one of his centralizing missions, came up against the independent spirit and resolute will of these robust peasants. "What is to be done with them?" he exclaimed in despair when met by the claims of "an impossible assembly of 'consuls' who return to their plough after casting aside their *'chaperons'* (the 'consul's' insignia)."

The period during which they exercised rule over their families is called in Provençal documents a "reign" . . . "en Olliol[2] (Ollioules) *renhava* ung mien reyregrand que si appelava Guilhem Deydier-Baralha." The Latin texts of the district of Briançon call these ruling peasants *"rois et chevaliers"*; *reges et milites.* We might think we were reading the Iliad or the Odyssey. "Heads of families were content to wear on *fête* days a good smock of the closely-woven homespun then in vogue, and another for working days of good linen with an old jacket underneath; maintaining their families in freedom and tranquillity, taking little interest in outside affairs beyond knowing how much wheat fetched in the market of the next village. . . ." In the evenings they might be seen "chatting freely together on some trifle or other, laughing heartily, telling stories of olden days *et neiges de l'année passée;* and on returning home from the fields everyone would have his broad jest with which to chaff his fellows, and incidents of the day to relate, each content with his lot and the calling which gave him an honest living. . . ." The above sketch is by good Noel du Fail, describing the types to be found in the sixteenth century. We have already given instances of these rural patriarchs cited by Retif; they did not disappear with the Revolution, and Mistral was able to give us a similar portrait of his father at the beginning of the nineteenth century:

Quite a crowd of retainers, some hired by the month and others as day labourers, would go to and fro over the land belonging to the *mas* (Provençal farm) with harrow and rake, or with a fork over their shoulder. . . . My

[2] "In Ollioules reigned one of my ancestors who was known as Guilhem Deydier-Batalha."

father dominated them by his height, by his good sense, and also by his noble birth. He was a fine and imposing type of an old man, dignified in his language, firm in his commands, benevolent to the poor and severe on himself alone. During the Revolution he engaged as a volunteer in defence of France, and in the evenings he would take pleasure in recounting his old battles. . . . My father had deep religious faith. At night time, summer or winter, he would pray aloud for us all, and when the evenings were long, he would read the Gospels to the children and servants.

As we see, it is just the same scene that took place under Edmond Retif's roof at Nitry in Burgundy. Mistral goes on:

My father used to celebrate Christmas with much ceremony, and after he had reverently blessed the logs on the hearth, he would speak to us of our ancestors, praising their lives, and praying for them. Whatever the weather he was always content, and if he sometimes heard people complaining about it on account of the high winds or torrential rain, he would say to them, "Good people, He who is up above knows quite well what He is doing, and what is good for us."

All his life he had worked and saved; but his table, like his purse, was open to every comer, and when any one was mentioned in his presence, he always asked whether he was a hard worker; and if they replied "Yes," he would say, "Then he is an upright man, and I am his friend."

He died like a patriarch. After he had received the last Sacraments all the household were weeping around his bed.

"Come, children!" he said, "I am going away, and I give thanks to God for all I owe to Him, for my long life and my labour which He has blessed."

Almost in every feature the above is also the faithful portrait of Retif de la Bretonne's father, as traced by his son.

We have already spoken of village weddings. It was a custom doubtless common in most of the French provinces — M. Dagnan-Bouveret has given us a delightful picture of it as still practised in the nineteenth century — for the bridegroom and bride-elect to kneel at the feet of the head of the family before proceeding to the church. All present knelt likewise. A prayer was recited aloud, and the father gave them his blessing, after which they left to the sound of violins to be married in the church.

In addition to the fine clothes of the bride, writes the Abbé de Marolles in the eighteenth century, and a head-dress of embroidery jingling with tinsel and glass beads, the relatives wore their well-pleated blue dresses which they would take out from their chests perfumed with lavender, dried roses and rosemary — I speak of the men as well as the women. . . . The wedding favours were not forgotten, each one wearing them at the waist or at the top of the sleeve. There would be the strains of pipes, flutes and hautbois, and afterwards a sumptuous banquet and rustic dances which lasted till the evening.

A red dress seems in most provinces to have been the bride's special "livery" just as white is to-day. The seigneur of the village, often a man of the highest rank, would take part in these rustic weddings. This was a tradition of which we have accurate record. The Duc de Croÿ writes, "we went to the house of the bride, where we saw preparations for a fine wedding feast laid for forty people consisting of only the the brothers and sisters of the two families; great store of turkeys and meat pies. We took one away with us and we danced with the bride. The Prince and Princess (de Condé) acted with quite good grace and in a popular spirit as was expected of them." This scene took place at Vanves.

WEALTH AND POVERTY OF THE RURAL CLASSES

We must not however draw a too favourable conclusion of prosperity from what has gone before. There is much authentic testimony showing the poverty which overtook the rural classes in one or other province after a bad harvest. The Ancien Régime could not bring great steamships from the New World, the East, or North Africa, laden with sufficient supplies to make up for the deficit due to the failure of the crops. The provincial customs houses, in maintaining which the people displayed the blindest obstinacy, were a further obstacle to the relief of the stricken districts; and so too was the violent hostility to the prudent provision that might have been made by the authorities beforehand to meet the exigencies of a possible food crisis. The economic notions of the period were still of a rudimentary kind, and the people were very severe towards speculators, or monopolists, to apply the term with which they were branded. With unreflecting prejudice the whole of France opposed "these monopolists who desolate the kingdom," against whom the Third Estate of Rheims was later on, in 1789, to demand the severest laws. Arthur Young, however, an experienced agriculturist, observes more justly, "It is necessary in order to secure a regular provision to give great encouragement to the monopolists."

Under conditions like these, poverty could not have failed to ensue after terrible winters such as those of 1709, 1740, 1767, 1771, 1775, 1784 and 1789, or in different parts of the country after a long drought. But the pictures drawn by Vauban, Massillon, the Marquis d'Argenson, and Arthur Young, of the distress of the agricultural classes in France before the Revolution, are much too darkly coloured. For instance, Vauban writes in his *Dîme Royale* (1707): "The evil has certainly gone too far, and if it be not remedied the people will fall into such extremities that they will never be able to recover." And yet the same writer declares in the same work that on Sundays and *fête* days the village taverns were never empty. He should be more consistent. The Marquis d'Argenson had been embittered by his disgrace and exile. We have, on the other hand, an equal number of rose-coloured descriptions to contrast with these darker views — Voltaire's for instance:

> I know not how it happens that in our villages, with an ungrateful soil, heavy taxes, and an intolerable prohibition against selling outside the district the wheat they have sown, there is hardly a single cultivator who does not possess a good cloth suit or is not well shod and well fed.

We have, too, the testimony of foreigners who judged our social conditions with no *arrière pensée;* for example, in 1739, Lady Montagu remarks upon "the air of abundance and contentment everywhere in the country districts of France," and Horace Walpole, as he passed through Artois in 1765, states, "I find this district thriving prodigiously . . . the smallest villages possess an air of prosperity." An Intendant of Roussillon takes note of the numerous meals eaten by the country folk, "four, five, even six daily, with meat and wine at every meal. . . ."

This varying testimony, however, cannot be taken as representative, either on one side or the other. . . .

THE DIVISION OF PROPERTY

The chief cause of the little progress realized in French agriculture from the sixteenth century, according to Arthur Young, who laid great stress on it, lay in the minute division of property: due partly to the equal distribution of an estate among the heirs, which was the general law for the greater portion of the rural classes; and partly to the fact that from the beginning of the second quarter of the eighteenth century the peasants were buying their land from the proprietors piece by piece, and in large numbers. The oft-repeated dividing up of the land among the cultivators was certainly a great benefit, but formed an obstacle to technical progress. On this point Arthur Young's showing is illuminating. According to him only a large landed proprietor has the means at his disposal to introduce new methods by reason of the cost entailed thereby, such as powerful machines doing the work of several men and giving a greater return. On small holdings where is there room for large pasture lands sufficient for a numerous head of cattle, which improve the strain and which provide a fertile source of manure? Only large proprietors have the means to break up the soil properly, to drain it, to bring waste ground into cultivation and to import artificial manures, often from a great distance. A large landed proprietor in Lancashire or Devonshire will import from Italy, Holland, and even from Normandy and Brittany, fresh stock of cattle, sheep, and pigs to improve his strain, whereas a small proprietor cannot even dream of doing so.

> Everywhere the peasants possess small properties [writes Young] to an extent we have no idea of in England; this is the case in all parts of the kingdom. . . . I have more than once seen this dividing up carried to such an excess that a single fruit tree on about 10 perches of land constituted a farm and the local situation of a family.
>
> The small farmer is powerless [concludes Young] and he is poor. He is in no condition to put forth the efforts required by good cultivation. . . . In a small farm division of labour is impossible; the same man does all the work of the farm in turns. On the larger farms there are labourers, threshers, hedgers, shepherds, cowmen, bullock drivers, pig men, lime burners, men to drain the land and others to water it; in this way the work must be done better on a large farm than on a small. One of the most useful things is a sheepfold; this can only be found on a large farm, otherwise the labour it entails absorbs all the profit.

This is just what was said in the 1739 reports of the Tiers Etat. That from Cernon (Marne, canton of Ecury-sur-Coole) states: "Although we are all owners, many of us are without the necessities, and hardly anyone possesses the means required for good farming."

Many holdings, according to Arthur Young, were so small that the owner had not enough to do to employ his time. Some did not consist of sufficient land for the employment and feed of a plough horse, and so the proprietor might be seen digging his field from one end to the other, after the advice of La Fontaine's worthy labourer to his children. Young noticed peasants at the foot of the mountains in Languedoc carrying earth in baskets on their backs, to form soil on the higher levels. "At Landivisau," writes the Englishman, "I saw a man who had tramped two-and-a-half leagues in order to take two chickens to market which, in my opinion, were not worth twenty-four *sous* for the pair. I came across people at Avranches, each with a horse, carrying about four bushels of sea-weed." Others ended by doing nothing at all; in order to occupy the time they would remove stakes from one place to another, and change the position of a bed of cabbages or turnips.

Another cause of the backward state of cultivation in France is shown in the agricultural associations at the end of the eighteenth century. We are referring to those vast stretches of land held in common, the exploitation of which was split up among the inhabitants of the village, and to those woods and fields the pasture of which was free; in other places there was marshy land where they would cut the reeds. A third obstacle to progress, according to academic opinion, lay in those admirable *maisons de village,* those associations of the different members of one large family of cultivators for the exploitation in common of their ancestral domain. Too rigorously attached to their traditional practices and customs, they hesitated to adopt new methods within their wide boundaries.

Yet another reason, according to Young and certain modern historians, would lie in the development and multiplication, from the year 1750, of rural manufactures, under the encouragement of the parish priests themselves.

Yet in spite of everything, the division of property, land held in common, *maisons de village,* and crafts giving work in the home, were, in a social sense, the greatest benefits that could be desired.

PROGRESS REALIZED IN THE EIGHTEENTH CENTURY

Whatever value may be attached to Arthur Young's judgment on French agriculture at the close of the Ancien Régime, it cannot be denied that, from the middle of the eighteenth century, it profited by the great movement drawing the whole of France towards a new future opening out for her by reason of the progress she had realized in every domain of national activity. The peasants were buying their land all over the country in a real passion for possession. The prices paid exceeded the value of the land; the rents of farms doubled; in the Marne Department they increased by two-thirds. Any land offered to rent at once found a tenant, and farmers soon found there was no more to be had. An increase in the value of leases followed: "From the middle of the eighteenth century till 1790 the rise became more accentuated," writes the Marquis d'Avenel, "and in the second half of the eighteenth century perhaps the most rapid upward movement ever remembered in our economic annals took place."

Under the influence of agricultural societies, and even of members of the aristocracy who took an interest in the cultivation of the land, many of the methods were improved, and agricultural machines were brought over from England; barns which cost so much to build were superseded by hay-stacks in the fields, and the growing of foodstuffs for the cattle increased to a very great extent. Arthur Young states that the cultivation of lucerne in France was on such a remarkable scale that his countrymen came over to our country to learn our methods. The introduction of maize, the rearing of silk-worms, the cultivation of the potato under the impulse given to it by Parmentier, and the Spanish breed of merino sheep acclimatized in our country by the labours of Daubenton, mark in France at the close of the Ancien Régime the achievement of victories of such importance that the nineteenth century can show nothing comparable to them. . . .

A POOR STATE IN A RICH COUNTRY

PIERRE GAXOTTE

Although the author of several books published over the last three decades dealing with different periods of French history, Pierre Gaxotte, unlike most of the other writers whose work appears in connection with this problem, has not generally engaged in original scholarly research. Possessed of a sharp, critical mind and a pleasing style, M. Gaxotte has successfully built upon the work of others. His keen intellect has, however, enabled him to synthesize a large amount of material in new and striking ways and he has received wide popular acclaim. The point of view expressed in his book on the Revolution from which the following is taken places him clearly in the conservative tradition.

DISTRESS may cause riots, but cannot produce revolutions. These latter are due to more deep-lying causes, and in 1789 the French were not in distress. On the contrary, there is most trustworthy documentary evidence that the country had considerably increased in wealth since the middle of the century and that, with the exception of the country gentry, the material condition of all classes of society had sensibly improved.

The system of corporations, which was much less oppressive and universal than has been assumed, had not prevented the growth and secure establishment of large industries. The use of machinery, which had been imported from England, had encouraged the concentration of capital, and some of the characteristic features of France as a mining and manufacturing country were already taking shape. In the north and on the fringe of the central plateau were coal mines and smelting furnaces (the Creusot works date from 1781); there was silk weaving at Lyons; there were cotton mills at Rouen and Mühlhausen; haberdashery was manufactured at Troyes; and woollen goods at Castres, Sedan, Abbeville and Elbeuf; Lorraine had iron and salt works; soap was made at Marseilles; while in Paris there were tanneries and manufactories of furniture and articles of luxury. There were already complaints about the scarcity of labour and the lack of fuel.

All the forms of business association usual at the present day were in current practice from that time onward. Nobles and *bourgeois* joined in financing them, and great lords became the sleeping-partners of commoners. The coal mines of Anzin and Aniche were the property of two joint-stock companies, one of which had been founded by the Prince de Croy. The Duc du Charost exploited Roche-la-Molière; the Prince de Conti, the Marshal de Castries et Tubeuf the Grand'Combe mines.

The modern figure of the great industrialist who keeps his millions on the move and has hundreds of workmen at his command was in existence long before the Revolution, just as were the financier, the middleman, the stock-jobber, the money-lender and the exchange-broker. There was a stock exchange; there were banks; there

Reprinted from *The French Revolution* by Pierre Gaxotte, translated by Walter Alison Phillips (1932) with the permission of Charles Scribner's Sons.

was the Caisse d'Escompte (the discount bank founded by Turgot in 1776), with a capital of a hundred millions, which issued notes similar to those of the Bank of France to-day; there was dealing in futures, quotation of prices, and gambling in stocks and shares. There was speculation in the exchanges, in State securities, in the companies interested in the farming of the indirect taxes (*Ferme générale*) and in the stocks of the great companies: the Compagnie des Indes, the Compagnie des Eaux and the Compagnie des Assurances. In the opinion of Necker, France had in her possession half the specie in Europe.

Foreign trade had made prodigious strides, and we are able – a rare thing in the economic history of the old regime – to follow these year by year, thanks to the statistics drawn up by Arnould, a clerk in the office of the Controller-General of the Finances, which are corroborated by the data collected by the Compagnie des Indes. This trade had more than quadrupled since the death of Louis XIV, and in 1788 it was valued at 1,061 millions of *livres*, an enormous figure which was not to be reached again before 1848.

The great ports – Marseilles, Bordeaux, Nantes – had all that animation, colour, cosmopolitan character and air of opulence and grandeur which even nowadays astonish the peasant from the interior, accustomed to narrow horizons and a quiet life. Marseilles monopolized the trade of the Levant. On its quays and in its warehouses were piled masses of carpets, printed cottons, liquors, rice, grain, Cyprus wines, oil, hides, muslins and printed calico. Bordeaux and Nantes had the monopoly of colonial wares, and San Domingo alone supplied half the sugar consumed in the world. The great ship-owners of these ports, whose position had been temporarily shaken by the Treaty of 1763, rapidly recovered their ground, and the victories won during the War of American Independence inspired them with fresh audacity. Where seven ships had been launched in 1738, thirty-three were built in 1784. The wines of Bordeaux found buyers as far off as Russia, and those of Burgundy reigned supreme in the Netherlands and Germany.

Internal trade followed a parallel course. In 1715 there were none but bad roads, interrupted by quagmires and ruined by floods, together with a few unevenly paved highways. By 1789 there were ten thousand leagues of good roads, solidly paved and kept up by a regular service, to which neither rivers nor mountains formed a barrier. The postal service, reorganized by Turgot, was more rapid and less expensive. In no other country was it possible to travel so quickly, so conveniently and at so small a cost. Arthur Young, who visited France under Louis XVI, when the Revolution was just beginning, is unstinted in his admiration for the beauty and convenience of the French roads, though for the rest he is much given to decrying everything that is not English.

At this point, however, a grave problem presents itself. Was this brilliant society, as has been affirmed, based upon a foundation of destitution? Was there an enormous mass of starving and poverty-stricken peasants beneath the gilded crowd of *bourgeois?* Many have asserted this, and have proceeded to quote La Bruyère's famous passage – "one sees certain wild animals, both male and female . . . black, livid and all scorched by the sun . . ." – without reflecting that this page, now a century old, was only a piece of fine writing trumped up by a sour moralist who, like all his contemporaries, regarded the charming valley of Chevreuse as a savage desert.

Frightful pictures of country life have also been gleaned from the works of the economists. But the greater number of these were drawn by men of sedentary habits, who only knew the country through the works of Quesnay, at a period when it was the fashion to celebrate the simple virtues of tillers of the soil and shed torrents of tears over a dearth of forage or the sad fate of merino sheep. The evidence of travellers has been cited, but every heart-rending observation which they have made may be balanced by another which contradicts it. How, indeed, is it possible to draw any general conclusion from these fleeting impressions? In the course of an hour's coaching one passes from a rich land into a poor one, from a fertile soil to a barren one. A day's hail-storms are enough to devastate a village. A crop which promises well in June may be miserable in July. A sunny spring may compensate for an abominable winter. Everything changes from year to year. Everything varies from province to province. In short, it would be rash to deduce from minor and strictly localized facts any conclusions applicable outside the limits of the canton in which they were noted.

Further, it is necessary to remember this indisputable fact of capital importance, namely, that the system of taxation which weighed on the peasant made the appearance of poverty an almost absolute necessity for him.

The *taille,* which was the most important of the rural imposts, was an income-tax roughly assessed on the basis of *the external evidence of wealth,* and the collectors were chosen in rotation from among the peasants themselves. For anyone subject to this tax to be honest and make accurate returns was, therefore, to court disaster; for the whole burden would have fallen upon him. The task of the tax-collectors was to get together a lump sum fixed in advance for the whole commune, and, in their eagerness to be rid of their horrid task as quickly as possible, they were only too glad to come across an honest simpleton whose quota they would naturally hasten to double and treble, while dealing gently with those from whom they anticipated difficulties, those who were astute enough to hide their incomes, the hot-heads who had a reputation for not allowing themselves to be put upon, and the hardened litigants who were not afraid of complications and "rows."

It was a dogma firmly fixed in the popular consciousness that the only way to avoid paying for other people, the only method by which it was possible to escape being crushed by unjust assessments, was to restrict expenditure, to appear to have no means, and to affect all the outward signs of the most utter destitution. "The richest man in a village," wrote the *grand bailli* of the Île-de-France in 1709, "would not dare to kill a pig at present except by night, for if he did so in public, his taxes would be increased." In the same way the provincial Assembly of Berry pointed out, in 1778, that the husbandman was afraid to let it be known what he earned, and refused to spend his income on "furniture, clothes, food, or anything that could be seen by other people. . . ."

It is the fate of arbitrary taxes, even when moderate in amount, to be hard to collect. The tax-payer of the old regime was restive, secretive and churlish, to a degree which it is hard for us to understand. His ill-will knew no bounds, and he only paid up when absolutely forced to do so. As often as not, he was two or three years in arrears. Boisguilbert says that a man who had a hidden store of money would not give up a *sou* until the fourth demand. Rather than admit, by paying in instalments, that he was in easy circumstances, he would prefer to be summoned before the courts and threatened with distraint. The intendant was harassed by protests and complaints. The lord of the manor, the judge and the parish priest were begged to intercede. People groaned, wept and protested incessantly, and those came off best who groaned, protested and wept loudest and longest so as not to appear richer and more easy to deal with than their neighbours.

Rousseau once lost his way in the mountains, and, being very hungry, went into a peasant's cottage and asked for something to eat. The man refused. He protested that he had nothing, that everything had been taken from him, that there was not a morsel of food, and that, search as he might, his cupboard was empty. Rousseau begged, insisted and mentioned his name. The other listened, grew calmer, and, being reassured, tremblingly opened a secret store from which, with an air of great mystery, he produced bread, meat and wine, protesting all the while that he would be lost "if anyone were to know that he possessed so much wealth."

This exactly describes the position of the peasants under the old regime. There was a great affectation of distress, but behind this cloak of rags was hidden a life that was tranquil, often easy, and sometimes ample.

The peasants, needless to say, were free men. Serfdom, which survived in nearly all the countries of Europe, had ceased to exist in France. It only lingered on, in a mitigated form, in certain corners of the Jura and the Bourbonnais. In 1779 the King had been at pains to abolish the last relics of it on his domains, and his example had been followed by certain lords in Franche-Comté.

The peasants were also as a rule the owners of their holdings. Whereas in England the system of enclosures had degraded them to the hard lot of servants and day-labourers, in France they had profited by the rise in the price of agricultural produce to better themselves. It is certain that on the eve of the Revolution they owned at least half the soil. Moreover, in the part owned by the clergy, nobles and *bourgeois* must be reckoned much unproductive land, such as woods, preserves, parks and pleasure grounds.

Some figures may here be cited by way of illustration. Between 1750 and 1789 the peasants of the *généralité* of Soissons had acquired four times the amount of land that they had lost. Between 1779 and 1781 those of Limousin had gained 4,000 *arpents*.[1] In eighty-five parishes of the *élection* of Tulle the peasants owned 137,080 out of 249,000 *arpents*. In forty-three parishes of the *élection* of Brive they owned 34,000 out of 63,000. In these two districts only 17 per cent of them did not own their holdings.

In the case of certain villages still more favourable conditions may be established, as, for instance, in the case of Gillonay, in Dauphiné, near the Côte-Saint-André. In 1702, out of 1,378 *hectares* the peasants owned 800. At the time of the Revolution they owned 1,250, the nobles having kept only a few vineyards. The two châteaux and their home farms had been sold to wealthy men of the middle class.

At Saint-Benoist-sur-Loire, in the Orléannais, from 1734 onward the famous old abbey, which had owned the whole countryside, retained only four farms. All the rest had been acquired by the farmers in easy circumstances — *laboureurs,* as they were then called — out of their savings. The remainder of the population, say some three hundred and forty heads of families, shared among them 733 *arpents* of arable lands, vineyards and pasturage. Two hundred and ninety-six of them owned houses or parts of houses. Of the four inhabitants mentioned as day-labourers or workmen, the first owned a house and garden, the second a piece of vineyard, the third an *arpent* of arable land and half an *arpent* of vineyard, the fourth half an *arpent* of land and a piece of vineyard.

The very small property-owners would farm two pieces of land at the same time, one on their own account and the other as farmers or *métayers*. And to this must be added yet another resource — home industries, such as weaving and the making of small metal-ware, which have now almost completely disappeared, but were very widespread in the eighteenth century. The locksmiths of Vimeu and the watchmakers of the Jura still bear witness to the existence of this former mode of labour.

In many places the methods of cultivation remained primitive. The practice of allowing the land to lie fallow was almost universal, and the yield of the harvests was poor. The Government, therefore, took pains to spread the use of scientific cropping and often succeeded, with the assistance of the great nobles, who, stimulated by the fashion for country pursuits, began to take a keen interest in agriculture.

[1] The *arpent* contains 100 square perches, the English acre 160; 4,000 *arpents,* therefore, equal 2,500 acres.

Model farms were established, veterinary schools founded, competitions organized, numerous marshes drained, moorlands brought under cultivation, common pasturage reduced, and cattle-breeding improved by the introduction and acclimatization of new strains. Goethe, who came to France in 1792 as the guest of the staff of the Prussian Army, was struck with the neatness and solidity of the houses in Lorraine, the beauty of their furniture and the rich contents of their cellars. If this cannot yet be called comfort, it was something very much resembling it.

But was this property of the peasants, which was increasing and improving, property in the full sense of the word, or was it merely a usufruct burdened with intolerable forms of servitude?

Feudalism, though no longer existing as a political system or even as the framework of society, survived as a civil and economic institution. Alongside the royal government were to be seen, cumbering the ground, the ruins of the government which had preceded it, which, though stripped of its powers and no longer rendering any services, continued to be paid for them. It is certain, and moreover natural and legitimate, that these charges, for which there was no longer any apparent reason, should not have been borne patiently. It is also obvious that they naturally appeared increasingly vexatious in proportion to the growth of the peasants' holdings. But whether they constituted an insupportable burden is more than doubtful. To begin with, we must not be led astray by the extraordinary number of words used to designate the feudal dues and services. No language had such a wealth of synonyms. According to the district, the amount payable or the nature of the land, the same seigniorial right could be called *champart, terrage, agrier, agrière, parcière, tasque, tierçage, sixte, cinquain, vingtain, carpot,* etc. Each substantive had seven or eight equivalents, and sometimes more, and from this infinity of appellations people jumped to the conclusion that a voracious fiscal system existed under a large variety of forms, whereas in reality everything came down to four or five dues, paid, some in kind, others in money.

The amount of the dues payable in money had been fixed once for all during the Middle Ages. This meant that, owing to the depreciation of the value of money, these payments had become purely nominal and survived as mere formalities, calculated, perhaps, to flatter the vanity of the lord of the manor, but not to fill his purse.

The dues in kind were more burdensome, but the title to them was contested, and many *seigneurs* abstained from any rigorous enforcement of their rights, through negligence, dislike of possible difficulties or fear that their peasants would emigrate elsewhere. "Make as much fuss as you like," wrote Duc de Cossé-Brissac to his agents, "but do not resort to compulsion except in urgent and indispensable cases."

In a number of places it was quite a usual thing for the peasants to remain twenty or thirty years without paying anything. In others arrangements had been made with them by which the old rates had been considerably reduced. In yet other cases, on purchasing their land they had also bought the dues to which it was subject. Hundreds of tolls (*péages*) had been abolished by the intendants. Though the *cens* – the money payment due to the *seigneur* – no longer had any reason for existing, the *banalités* were still justified by the equivalent services rendered by the lord's wine press, bakery and mill. Similarly the tithes paid to the Church implied an obligation on the part of the clergy to bear the charges of public worship, to teach the children, minister to the poor and nurse the sick.

Truth to tell, it was not their burdensomeness that made the survivals of feudalism hateful, but the simple fact that they *were* survivals, with all the uncertainties and disputes that this entailed. "There is," said Le Trosne, "nothing real in feudalism except the law-suits." And as a matter of fact this was the whole trouble.

Feudal dues provided a never-ending pretext for chicanery. A swarm of petty country attorneys, for whom these vexatious proceedings provided the only means of livelihood, employed themselves with unerring skill in fomenting trouble. Everything was a pretext for a dispute: the obscurity of the customs, the vague terms, the absence of original title-deeds, the difficulty of finding equivalents for the old superficial measures and those of capacity, the discrimination between what was due in money and what was not, the number, nature and legitimacy of changes of ownership and repurchases, the frauds and delays of the seigniorial millers, etc. Again and again the same cases were argued before the courts, lawsuits following each other without respite or cessation. The parties would vie with each other in bad faith in order to avoid a settlement, and in this the judge would aid and abet them.

This rage for disputes and litigation grew worse and worse in the latter half of the eighteenth century. First there was the sharing-out of the communal lands, which set everybody by the ears. Then many of the *seigneurs*, feeling that they no longer possessed unassailable title-deeds now that their pretensions were being attacked more and more every day, started having their muniments (*terrier*) revised, verified and completed by lawyers who had made a special study of this kind of work, to whom they usually allowed a percentage on the rents which they succeeded in recovering.

The peasants, who had always pleaded the insufficiency of the deeds as justification for their resistance, could not but lose by this operation. At the very time when the Government was proposing through the publicists in its pay the abolition of the rights from which they were suffering, the peasants felt that the *seigneurs* were attempting to lay new and crushing burdens upon them, and so rose against them with the desperation of a drowning man who meets with an unforeseen obstacle when on the point of reaching the shore.

There was really no justification for this hatred. Generally speaking, the squires were not bad fellows. As dirty and mud-stained as their farmers, they retained hardly anything of their lordly estate save a genealogical tree, a dove-cote, a sporting dog and an old rusty sword. Their fortunes had foundered in the storms of the wars of religion, and the constant rise in the cost of living, caused by the influx of American gold, had made it impossible to restore them. Like Chateaubriand's father, who lived with five servants and two mares in a castle which could have housed a hundred knights with their followers and King Dagobert's pack of hounds, they lived but poorly in their decayed and empty manor houses. More often than not, the last remnants of their lands were mortgaged and their rents pledged to business men, who collected them with a harshness which they themselves would never have used.

The peasants had no reason to hate them personally. In many places they were to protect and save them at the very height of the Terror. But in the year 1788 they had a grudge against them for being the last obstacle to their own complete enfranchisement. And the last obstacle was the one against which rage and resentment beat with accumulated force, and which was savagely broken down in the hurry to reach the goal, instead of being got round as the others had been. The shadow of servitude often seems a greater burden than servitude itself.

The countryside, like the towns, had grown richer, though less strikingly so. The whole of France had shared in the growing prosperity. In the absence of other evidence, this fact would be sufficiently proved by the regular growth of the population. This numbered 25 millions, which was double that of England or Prussia, and equal to that of Germany, Austria and Hungary combined. . . .

THE PEASANTS AND AGRICULTURE

HENRI SÉE

Because of ill-health, Henri Sée had to retire from active teaching at the University of Renes in 1920. He was able, however, to carry on his research and publication and made many contributions to our knowledge of the economic history of both France and Europe before his death in 1936. Originally trained as a medievalist he tended to concentrate on economic problems. Among other achievements he has provided us with several valuable studies of French economic developments during the Old Regime. A firm partisan of objective history, he attempted to hold himself aloof from scholarly dispute as the moderate and judicious views set forth in the following selection will show.

FIRST we shall describe the classes that live from real property, that is, land, either by deriving their resources from agricultural labor (the peasants), or by living from the exploitation of the peasants, in other words, from the revenues which the peasants are obliged to furnish those who are the eminent proprietors of the soil, namely, the clergy and the nobility.

The first step, then, is to get an idea of the apportionment of property among these three social classes. Doubtless we cannot secure precise statistics. We can only, by virtue of tax-lists and especially the rolls of twentieths (*vingtièmes*), which Loutchisky has used, and also by virtue of the numerous land-records of the eighteenth century, make computations that are, to be sure, merely approximate, yet throw light upon the facts and are in accord with actual realities.

The figures that we shall quote have no absolute value. They can be criticised severely and may be modified by further investigations. On the other hand, since they are based upon voluminous abstracts of tax-lists, the details of which Loutchisky was not always able to give, it seems legitimate to use them. On the whole we believe they have a real value, in spite of the criticisms directed against them.

THE PROPERTY OF THE PRIVILEGED CLASSES

It appears that the nobility possessed an important part of the land, but a much smaller amount than was usually believed. In his work "Etat des classes agricoles à la veille de la Révolution" (Condition of the Agricultural Classes on the Eve of the Revolution) Loutchisky arrives at the following conclusions: in Artois the nobility had 29 per cent of the land; in Picardy 33 per cent; in Burgundy 35 per cent; in Limousin 15 per cent; in Upper Auvergne 11 per cent; in Quercy 15 per cent; in Dauphiné 12 per cent; in Landes 22 per cent; in Béarn 20 per cent; in the section of Toulouse 28 per cent; in Roussillon 32 per cent; in Orléanais about 40 per cent. In Upper Brittany and Normandy and generally in western France the holdings of the nobility seem to have been much more extensive than in the other regions.

Contrary to what was long believed, the

clergy owned infinitely less land than the nobility. Northern France is an exception in this respect. Thus in Hainault and Cambrésis the clergy held 40 per cent of the property, and in Artois the ecclesiastical holdings comprised one-fifth or one-fourth of the land, while in Laonnois these holdings amounted to 29 per cent and in Picardy to 18 per cent. But the farther west or south we go, the smaller the proportion grows, as the following table reveals:

	Per cent
Burgundy	11 and 15
Berry	15
Touraine	10
Auvergne	3.5
Lower Limousin and Quercy	2
Section of Toulouse	4
Roussillon	2.5
Béarn	1.5
Landes	1
Section of Rennes	3.4

As for the total, we may agree with G. Lecarpentier, who ascribes to the clergy an average of only 6 per cent of the land of France. The wealth of the clergy, as we shall see, was due in great part to its urban holdings and the collection of tithes.

It should also be noted that a large proportion of the property of the nobility and the clergy consisted of small forests and woods, and that these holdings were usually divided into small parcels—a fact which made agricultural exploitation on a large scale, in accordance with the English practise, impossible. It is well to note that when we speak of the property of the nobility and the clergy, we mean only the immediate land of the manors (the so-called *domaine proche*) which was usually rented to farmers, or *métayers*, farming on half profits. But the lords exercised also a right of eminent ownership over the lands dependent upon their fiefs and especially upon the peasant tenures, for very few of the latter were allodial, that is, completely autonomous.

PEASANT PROPERTY

It is nevertheless true that the peasant tenures should be regarded as real hereditary property, since they were willed to heirs or could be transferred. They were merely encumbered by dues and taxes collected by the lord. Hence the peasants possessed a considerable part of the land, the proportion of which, however, varies in the different sections. In the western provinces it seems smallest. Thus in Normandy, Brittany, and Poitou we estimate it at only about one-fifth. In the north, in Picardy, in Artois, and in the region that later formed the Département du Nord (Flanders, Hainault and Cambrésis), as well as in Orléanais and Burgundy, it amounts to about one-third. In Languedoc and Limousin it is one-half, and in Dauphiné it is two-fifths. In the second half of the eighteenth century, peasant property, far from decreasing, seems to have undergone a notable increase in certain regions. Loutchisky finds this true generally of Soissons, where the peasants acquired four times as much land as they sold, as well as of Limousin, where from 1779 to 1791 they acquired an additional four thousand acres. Nevertheless Lefebvre thinks he can prove that peasant holdings in the north hardly increased after 1770; only the number of owners grew during the eighteenth century, no doubt as the result of inheritance. However that may be, since the peasants constituted 90 per cent of the owners, their holdings were often very small. The small size of the peasant holdings is an undeniable fact and one of great importance.

Many peasants possessed only infinitesimal parcels of land, particularly in northern France. Lefebvre proves that in Cambrésis from 60 to 70 per cent of the owners held less than a hectare, and 20 per cent less than five hectares. But since at least five hectares are necessary to support a family, most of the peasants had to find work as farmers or as agricultural laborers. In Flanders, Cambrésis, and Hainault, as well as in Artois, Picardy, and Normandy, and to a certain extent in Britanny, there was a veritable rural proletariat which was reduced to misery by lack of work or poverty, and that explains the great number of beggars and vagabonds. Owners of means and farmers on a large scale (often called *laboureurs*) constituted only a small minority of the rural population. It was especially this class that, at the time of the Revolution, profited by the abolition of the manorial system and the sale of the national property.

The bourgeoisie, too, owned a considerable portion of the real property, especially near the towns and larger cities, where there was a greater field for activity. In the north, for example, from 16 to 17 per cent of the land was owned by the bourgeoisie.

This distribution of the real property which we have outlined gives France of the eighteenth century a quite peculiar aspect. It distinguishes the country notably from England, where the great holdings of the nobility gradually did away with small peasant holdings, because of the enclosures. It distinguishes France also from the greater part of central Europe, and particularly from eastern Europe, where the large holdings of the nobility continually extended and grew stronger in the course of modern times. This phenomenon has given to French society an original character and has exercised a notable influence upon its entire historical development.

The agrarian development of England since the end of the Middle Ages shows us the reasons why peasant ownership was preserved and strengthened in France. In Great Britain the progress of the wool industry inspired the lords to transform cultivated lands into pasturages and to increase their immediate domain by means of enclosures. And at the same time the greater precariousness of the tenures, which had made itself felt since the Middle Ages, as well as the weakening of the manorial system, facilitated this transformation. The British lords were not interested in maintaining the peasant tenures, which netted them only small revenues. Finally the aristocracy, which had seized the political power as a result of the revolutions during the seventeenth century, was free to take possession of all the land. In France it was quite different. Commercial and industrial capitalism was slower to develop and less intense. The lords were increasingly submitted to the authority of the crown, which opposed excessive encroachments. Furthermore, since they enjoyed extensive manorial rights that were often lucrative, the nobles did not care to destroy the system of peasant tenures depending upon their fiefs. Thus small peasant ownership perhaps owes its continued existence and its progress to the maintenance of the manorial system. And then, when the Revolution destroyed this system, peasant ownership finally became fully autonomous. . . .

AGRICULTURAL EXPLOITATION

Few large parcels, a predominance of exploitation on a small scale, and cultivation in the hands of the poor peasants—these are some of the conditions that militate against the progress of agriculture. In fact, French agriculture was at this time quite backward, especially if we compare it with English agriculture.

One characteristic feature was the great quantity of uncultivated lands and waste-lands, especially in Brittany, where they comprised two-fifths of the area, and in the mountainous regions, such as Roussillon, the Central Chain (*Massif Central*) and the Alpine regions. To be sure, the proportion was much smaller in the Îsle de France, in Picardy, Flanders and Alsace. The uncultivated lands play an important part in the rural economy of the period. Many peasants without pasturage sent their cattle to graze on the common waste-lands and used the produce of these lands as litter for their animals, and especially as fertilizer for their fields.

The methods of cultivation remained very primitive, and progress was very slow, except in the richest and most fertile regions. The farm-buildings were poorly arranged, and the implements were unsatisfactory and quite primitive, being hardly superior to those employed during the Middle Ages. Intensive cultivation was practically unknown almost everywhere. The system of fallow land was used universally, except in Flanders, Alsace, and a part of Normandy. Even in Picardy the land lay idle one year in three. In Brittany it was left idle every other year, sometimes for two years out of three, and certain "cold" lands were cultivated only every seven or eight years, or even every twenty years. The artificial meadow was hardly ever used.

The peasants, prompted by the spirit of routine and having but little capital, devoted no great care to cultivation. They did not plow deeply, they weeded their grain negligently, sowed too late, and used poor seed. Almost everywhere there was lack of good manure. Since the farm itself furnished very little manure, leaves and ferns, allowed to rot, were used instead. This explains the small crops. In Brittany they hardly exceeded 5 or 6 to 1; in Limousin 3 or 4, while in Flanders they rose exceptionally to 11.

Another characteristic feature was that in almost all France wheat was considered a luxury crop and rye predominated, except in Toulouse, Angoumois, and the coastal region of Brittany. Poor land was used particularly for buckwheat, and this furnished the peasants their principal nourishment in the form of cakes. In the central and southern sections maize played an important part. Flax and hemp were more extensively cultivated than is the case today, because of the extent of rural and domestic industry. The government, fearing that wines might take the place of grains, restricted the cultivation of the former in the eighteenth century. But it flourished and was remunerative in the south and particularly in Lower Languedoc. Forest exploitation, ruined by a poor system of management and by abuses on the part of the commoners, left much to be desired, and the development of the ironworks, mines and foundries increased deforestation, which became more and more serious. Cattle-raising and horse-breeding remained very mediocre, although the second half of the eighteenth century witnessed a certain amount of improvement.

Carelessness on the part of the great proprietors, the indolence of the peasants, who were discouraged by the overwhelming taxes, insufficiency of the ways of communication and particularly of the main highways, in addition to obstacles placed in the path of the trade in agricultural commodities and in the path of free cultivation — all these things explain the slow development of agriculture.

During the second half of the eighteenth century efforts were, indeed, made to improve agricultural conditions, but the initiative was taken almost exclusively by the government.

Under the influence of the economists, and particularly the physiocrats, agriculture became one of the most important considerations of the royal administration. Memorials and instructions were continually sent to the governors of the provinces recommending improved methods in agriculture. The first agricultural committee was created in 1761, and Bertin, who from 1761 to 1783 seems to have been a veritable minister of economic affairs, initiated a whole series of measures for increasing the productiveness of the soil. Toward the end of the *ancien régime,* as a result of the drought of 1785, a committee for the administration of agriculture was created, having among its members some very distinguished scholars, agriculturists and economists, such as Lavoisier, the botanist du Tillet, the economist Dupont de Nemours, the inspector of factories Lazowski, and Duke de la Rochefoucauld-Liancourt. These men made interesting investigations and drew up very instructive reports, but their activities extended over only two years, from 1785 to 1787.

Since 1761 Bertin had endeavored to establish in each generality an agricultural society. The estates of Brittany had founded one as early as 1757. These societies made interesting investigations, and their members drew up reports and even conducted experiments. But their efforts, which extended over only a few years, do not seem to have had a great effect upon the progress of agriculture. The great majority of the planters remained faithful to the traditional practises, especially on account of lack of capital. Only in the rich sections of the northwest was appreciable progress noted. Artificial meadows were developed there and new crops introduced.

It is true that in the kingdom as a whole the amount of productive lands increased. The royal declarations of 1764 and 1766 encouraged, by exemption from taxation, the draining of the marshes and the clearing of the uncultivated lands. Indeed important sections were drained in Picardy, Normandy, Brittany and Vendée. Many uncultivated lands were cleared in all sections. However, on the eve of the Revolution the main part of the work still remained to be done. For the mass of the population, needing the waste-lands for its own uses, was opposed to draining and clearing, and for the same reason there was opposition to the division of the common property. In fact, such division was not very usual before the Revolution, as shown by the documents published by Georges Bourgin.

Division of the commons, draining and clearing seemed advantageous only to the great proprietors and such farmers as were in easy circumstances. They alone reacted favorably to the efforts of the government, undertaken during the last twenty years of the *ancien régime,* to restrict common pasture and the right of commonage, practises that were quite injurious to agriculture. It was found necessary to resort to partial measures, applicable only to regions in which reform seemed most urgent. Even these measures were not entirely effective.

There was a genuine need for a complete redistribution of lands, analogous to the system of enclosures which at that time was practised in England. But this was out of the question in France.

RURAL INDUSTRY

An indication of the insufficiency of agricultural production is the extension of rural industry in the seventeenth, and especially the eighteenth, century. This furnished an important addition to the means of subsistence of the peasant. We find it to be the case particularly in Brittany and Lower Maine. In Brittany the cloth industry was exclusively rural and domestic. Those engaged in it were the small proprietors, farmers (who often employed their servants), and day-laborers, who manufactured cloth when they had no work. The wages of the weavers were very small and the profits went largely to the manufacturers, that is, the merchants, who took up the finished product and often advanced the raw materials.

In regions where agriculture was more prosperous, as in western Normandy, Picardy, and Flanders, the peasants engaged in rural industry were those who possessed too little land to live from agriculture. In eastern Normandy the Parliament of Rouen, in 1722, speaks of peasants abandoning the cultivation of the soil in order to spin and card cotton, and it complains of the injurious result for agriculture. There was no Norman village without its spinners and weavers. Some 180,000 persons were thus employed by the industry at Rouen.

Picardy presented a quite similar picture.

In those provinces in which industry to some extent turned the cities toward the rural sections, the rural artisan was more closely bound to the class of merchants who took up his products and furnished him not only with the raw material, but even with the loom. In this case rural industry appears indeed to have been the first stage of development leading to the triumph of the great capitalist industry. In the rural sections of Upper Normandy and near Troyes the looms of the cotton trade did great damage to the workmen in the cities, who complained to the manufacturers that they were being reduced to misery. Because of mechanical improvements the weaver's trade was within reach of rather unskilled artisans without professional training and commanding very low wages, a fact which inspired the merchants all the more to avail themselves of their labor.

MODE OF LIFE AMONG THE PEASANTS

The material existence of the peasants was still quite miserable, even at the end of the *ancien régime*. Their dwelling-places were altogether inadequate. Most of them were built of mud, covered with thatch, and having only a single low room without a ceiling. The windows were small and had no glass. In Brittany, and especially in Lower Brittany, it has been said that the peasants lived "in the water and in the mud." This is one of the principal causes for the epidemics that were still so frequent. However, as today, living conditions varied in different regions. In northern France the peasants seemed to have the most comfortable homes.

Furthermore, we must never fail to distinguish between the peasants in comfortable circumstances and the poor ones, particularly when we consider furniture and clothing. The former had furnishings that were simple, primitive and suitable, sufficient dishes and linen, as well as enough clothing. The poor, on the other hand, could hardly satisfy their most elementary requirements. Among the well-to-do the inventory after death — our principal source of information — sometimes estimates the furnishings at over one thousand *livres;* among the poor they are frequently worth no more than 50 or even 20 *livres*. The poor dispose of only one or two trunks, a table, a kneading-trough, a bench, and a roughly hewn bed. Among the farmers in good circumstances we find well made beds, wardrobes, all sorts of household utensils, bowls of wood or earthenware, pottery, and glasses. In clothing we also find great variety, from very good to very poor. Working clothes were almost always of canvas. Many peasants had only wooden shoes, or went barefoot, especially in the south. Heavy taxes on skins made shoes very expensive.

The food of the peasants was always coarse, and often insufficient. Meat appeared on the table but rarely. Sometimes they ate bacon. Except in sections where wine was plentiful, water was the usual beverage. In Brittany cider was drunk only in years of abundance. The basic foods were bread, soup, dairy products, and butter. Wheat bread was quite rare; only bread of rye and oats, and that frequently of poor quality, was known. In the poorest regions the peasants ate biscuits and porridge of buckwheat, or even of chestnuts or maize. Wheat and even rye served largely to pay the taxes and farm-rent, or were sold for export when this was permitted. Potatoes, which later became a staple food-product among the farmers, were grown only in a few particularly fertile regions, as for example in certain parts of the coastal region of Brittany.

Clothes were often wretched. The description of Besnard in "Souvenirs d'un nonagénaire" probably is accurate:

> The clothing of the poor peasants — and they were almost all poor — was even more pitiful, for they had only one outfit for winter and summer, regardless of the quality of the material. And their single pair of shoes, very thin and cleated with nails, which they procured at the time of their marriage, had to serve them the rest of their lives, or at least as long as the shoes lasted.

The women "wore a short cloak of coarse material or black caddis, to which was attached a hood for enveloping the head and neck in case of rain or cold." This description agrees pretty well with the reports of the inventories.

CRISES AND MISERY

If we would form an idea of the mode of life of the peasants, we must also distinguish between normal periods and critical times caused by foreign wars or bad crops.

In the eighteenth century the crises were less grave but no less frequent than in the seventeenth century. Certain provinces had directly borne the brunt of war, as for example Lorraine and Burgundy, which suffered terrible ravages, especially during the first half of the seventeenth century. Around Dijon, as Gaston Roupnal shows, entire villages were depopulated and the fields were left uncultivated.

Even under the personal government of Louis XIV, which is usually praised as having been very prosperous, there was great suffering in the rural sections of every part of France. In 1675 Lesdiguières, governor of Dauphiné, wrote:

> It is a fact, and I assure you that I know whereof I speak, that the great majority of the inhabitants of this province lived during the winter only from acorns and roots, and that now they can be seen eating the grass of the fields and the bark of the trees.

After 1685 the misery even increased. In 1687 Henri d'Aguesseau and Anton Lefèvre d'Ormesson, making an investigation in Maine and around Orléans, declared:

> There are practically no peasants in comfortable circumstances. There are only poor coöperative farmers who have nothing. The landlords have to furnish them with cattle, lend them food, pay their *taille,* and take their crops in payment, and often even this does not cancel the debt. . . . The peasants live from buckwheat bread. Others, who have no buckwheat, live from roots of ferns boiled with the flour of barley or oats, and salt. . . . One finds them sleeping on straw. They have no clothing except what they wear, and that is very poor. They are destitute of furnishings and provisions. Everything in their huts points to dire need.

In 1684 the ambassador of Venice declared: "I have seen with my own eyes sections that formerly had 700 or 800 homes, now reduced to 30 by the continual passage of troops of war."

During the last fifteen years of the reign of Louis XIV the misery grew more serious. The winter of 1709 witnessed a veritable famine.

All these facts must be taken into consideration if we would realize that during the last twenty-four years of the *ancien régime* there was, so far as these matters are concerned, undeniable improvement. During the eighteenth century the theatre of hostilities was almost always located beyond the frontiers, and there were fewer wars than during the era of the Great King. Nevertheless, there were great crises in 1725, 1740, 1759, from 1766 to 1768, from 1772 to 1776, in 1784 and 1785, and in 1789. Prices of food increased enormously. In 1785 the great drought compelled the farmers to sell a part of their cattle. In 1774 and again in 1789 the farmers had to live from turnips, milk, and even grass. In these critical years the day-laborers especially were affected, since they had nothing but the strength of their arms to depend upon.

But perhaps we should not paint the picture in too lurid colors. There were regions where agriculture was more prosperous, such as Flanders, Picardy, Normandy and Beauce, where the peasants were better off. This will be better understood when new monographs have been published. At present the best impression of this condition is given by Arthur Young's "Travels in France." This English economist observes the contrast that exists between the various regions. He notes the prosperity of sections where the land is cultivated mostly by small proprietors. Coming from Spain to France, he admires the prosperity of Béarn:

> Here, without passing a city, a barrier, or even a wall, we enter a new world. From the poor, miserable roads of Catalonia we suddenly reach a splendid highway built with all the substantial quality and excellence that characterize the great highways of France. In place of beds of torrents, there are well constructed bridges. From a rude desert region we come suddenly into a country of agriculture and progress.

All in all, we may say that there was more prosperity, relatively at least, in the rural sections, especially after 1750. And yet the peasant at the time of the outbreak of the Revolution had a keener feeling for his suffering. The reason is perhaps, as has been well said, that "the very alleviation of his misery made him feel all the more acutely what remained of it. Perhaps he was disgusted with the present by the new ideas and hopes that had made their way even into the rural sections."

EPIDEMICS, MENDICITY, AND AID

A consequence of the misery and bad living conditions are the frequent epidemics, which, although less dreadful than those of the Middle Ages, were none the less quite fatal. Measles and especially small-pox, typhus and typhoid fever claimed thousands of victims. In Brittany alone, during the year 1741, there were 80,000 deaths. It is a curious fact that the epidemics were more frequent and more formidable in the rural sections than in the cities. This is commented upon by the physicians of the period, and particularly by Dr. Bagot of Saint-Brieuc, in his "Observations médicinales" (Medical Observations). The peasants were almost entirely without medical attention. Only toward the end of the *ancien régime* did the government organize medical assistance, distributing remedies and appointing physicians in charge of epidemics.

Mendicity and vagrancy became veritable scourges against which the government was powerless. Especially in the rural sections the beggars and tramps were numerous. At critical times the day-laborers, reduced to misery, increased the number of these unfortunates. Many sought refuge in the cities, thinking that they would secure aid there. But the cities were no better off than the country.

In the face of this misery private charity was of no avail. Public assistance, organized in the cities, became increasingly inefficient in the country. Hospitals and charitable institutions, until then rather common, gradually disappeared. For example, in the section of Rennes, Fougères, and Vitré, at the end of the *ancien régime*, there remained hospitals in only three out of 140 parishes. For feeding the poor there were, generally speaking, only small foundations. The parish clergy took pity on the unfortunates, but generally there were no resources available. The rich abbeys did not respond as much as might have been expected. Hence the state was obliged to do what it could. Serious efforts were made by ministers who were reformers, such as Turgot and Necker. Charitable workshops were established to help the poor, and stations for distributing alms. But at the approach of the Revolution only insignificant results had been achieved, and the question, now having assumed serious proportions, was brought before the Constituent Assembly, which elected a Committee on Mendicity.

AGRARIAN TROUBLES

Usually the rural population passively endured the charges that oppressed them. It is a curious fact that there were real insurrections only during the reign of Louis XIV, whose authority, it is usually claimed, was so absolute. And these insurrections took place precisely during the years that were the most prosperous of his entire reign. The peasants rebelled against the establishment of new taxes or the increase of old ones. In 1662 Boulonnais, the section around Boulogne, rebelled. In spite of ancient privileges, Louis XIV had wished to impose upon the province, as he says in his *Mémoires,* "a very small sum," which "produced a bad effect." Six thousand persons took up arms, and the revolt was harshly repressed. In 1664 trouble arose in Béarn and Bigorre when the salt-tax was introduced. It lasted for several years, and the entire section was up in arms. In 1670 the absurd rumor spread in Vivarais that according to an edict a tax was to be levied on all births, clothes, and new hats. The whole section around Aubenas, some twenty parishes in all, rose under the leadership of Antoine du Roure.

When at the outbreak of the war with Holland in 1675, Colbert had to create new taxes (stamped paper, increase of the salt-tax, monopoly in tobacco, etc.), the section of Guyenne rebelled and the government mobilized two hundred companies to repress the insurrection. At the same time a part of Lower Brittany rebelled for the same reason. A certain number of parishes drew up what was known as the Peasant Code, a whole program of claims, and a sort of forerunner of the memorials of 1789. In fact the insurrection began to assume the proportions of a peasant revolt in defiance of the nobility. As is shown by the historian Jean Lemoine, who has written an excellent study upon the revolt over the stamped paper, the means of repression were terrible. The revolting peasants were hanged, and the troops proceeded to kill and pillage. All these insurrections seem to have been spontaneous. As Ernest Lavisse remarks very accurately, "In the case of these 'emotions,' which arise for the same reasons and at the same time in different places, there is no understanding necessary between the various sections. Brittany and Guyenne, Rennes and Bordeaux, each acted independently, without knowledge of the actions of the others. The individual conflagrations did not unite into a single flame."

It is interesting to note that during the eighteenth century, which is generally regarded as an era of decadence so far as the royal authority is concerned, there were no peasant uprisings comparable with the troubles that marked the reign of the Great King. The rural sections generally remained calm, either because the economic conditions were better than in the seventeenth century, as the quite considerable increase in population tends to prove, or because the provincial administration was better organized, and police protection was more efficient. Only just before the Revolution were there uprisings, caused by fear of famine because of the exportation of grain. And even so the government took measures to prevent suffering or to ward off its effects, by buying grain, subventioning the importers of grain and distributing it gratuitously or at a low price. Serious agrarian troubles arose only at the time of the Revolution, on the day after the 14th of July, and after the night of August 4, when the peasants wanted to secure the abolition of the hated manorial system, the suppression of which had been promised by the bourgeoisie.

. . . . . .

THE PEASANT QUESTION AND PUBLIC OPINION

The reforms made by the Convention were destined to be radical, since they abolished all manorial rights without indemnity. The question was settled forever.

But the revolutionary agitation was prepared by a powerful movement of public opinion, which appeared particularly during the second half of the eighteenth century. The physiocrats considered that the manorial system, because of all its harassing obstacles, was harmful to the progress of agricultural production. But their claims in this matter were of a very abstract nature.

However, the kings of Sardinia, by their edicts of 1762, 1771 and 1778, freed the peasants of Savoy of mortmain and decreed the abolition of the manorial dues. Hereupon Voltaire was encouraged to carry on his campaign in favor of the serfs of Franche-Comté with more zeal. In one of his memorials he recalls that "the king of Sardinia has freed all lands in Savoy of real and personal mortmain."

Then in 1776 there appeared the celebrated pamphlet of Boncerf on "The Disadvantages of the Feudal Rights," secretly encouraged by Turgot. In spite of his extreme moderation — he demanded obligatory redemption only in the case of the successors of the present lords, — he was condemned by the Parliament of Paris. Voltaire adhered fully to the ideas of Boncerf and arose vigorously against the Parliament, denouncing its egotism:

> To propose the abolition of the feudal rights is tantamount to attacking the holdings of the gentlemen of the Parliament themselves, most of whom possess fiefs. These gentlemen are therefore personally interested in protecting, defending and encouraging respect for the feudal rights. It is the case of the church, the nobility and the members of Parliament. These three classes, too often opposed to one another,

should unite against the common enemy. The Church will excommunicate those authors who may undertake the defense of the people, and will burn the authors as well as their writings. And by these means the writings will be victoriously refuted.

Jean Jacques Rousseau also did much to make the cause of the peasants popular. In the "Nouvelle Héloise," which enjoyed such a great measure of success, he steadfastly contrasts the artificial luxury of Paris with the simple and sound customs of the country folk. Saint Preux, traveling in Valais, admires the comfort and happiness of the mountaineers. He says: "Food is abundant, without any market toward the outside, and without any show of luxury within; nor does the mountaineer planter, whose work is his pleasure, become less industrious on that account."

The true genius of the French people Rousseau finds not in Paris, but in the provinces and remote rural sections.

The feeling for nature which he helped so much to disseminate attracted the attention of the city inhabitants to the rural population. The novel and the theatre began to depict in an idealistic and somewhat misleading, insipid fashion, the rural customs. In the "Tales" of Florian we meet only shepherds and shepherdesses. Marie Antoinette at Trianon posed as a farmer's wife. Although we should not ascribe to these manifestations of what would today be called a new form of snobbishness, more importance than they deserve, yet we should remember that to a certain extent they reveal the tendencies of a period.

OVERWHELMING IMPORTANCE OF THE PEASANT QUESTION

The peasant question was bound to be of importance in a country in which the rural population was numerically so important, where industry on a large scale was only in its infancy, and where agricultural production was more important than all other branches. Vauban had already said that "the real wealth of a kingdom lies in the abundance of its supply of food, which is so necessary for human life." Furthermore the population of a country, and its rural population in particular, is one of its greatest assets. In the eighteenth century the interest which intelligent officials, as well as economists, took in agricultural questions, attracted attention to the condition of that class which alone tilled the soil. In England during the same period it was the commercial and industrial questions that attracted public notice more than anything else.

THE CRISIS IN THE FRENCH ECONOMY AT THE END OF THE OLD REGIME

C. E. LABROUSSE

Unquestionably the leading French authority on the economic history of the Old Regime and the Revolution, C. E. Labrousse has been a pioneer in applying the latest economic and statistical theories of the business cycle and the interaction of multiple economic factors to historical studies and especially to the problem of the economic origins of the Revolution. Aware of the dangers and limitations of fragmentary evidence in generalizing about economic phenomena, he has conscientiously pursued his research at the most basic level and has sought to bring to bear a mass of data on any problem he attacks. On the other hand the relatively short excerpt which follows will certainly impress the reader with M. Labrousse's ability to generalize from his detailed data in a striking and effective manner.

THIS work is a study of a depression of moderately long duration and the shorter term crisis which followed it, and the causes and consequences of these. The depression covered the last part of the Old Regime, extending from about 1778 to 1787. The crisis, which developed after a brief recovery, reached its height in 1789 and lasted through the first quarter of 1790. . . .

Initially it was intended to do very much less: The present study was to have been limited to the economic crisis of 1789, or rather to the five-year cycle of decline which it dominated, that is to say, the period 1787–1789. It was not possible, however, to limit it to that. The collapse of 1789 could not be understood if isolated from the long period of uncertainty and depression which preceded it. The gravity of the illness in 1789 resulted in large measure from the fact that it attacked an organism which was already very anemic.

Economic anemia in the 18th century? Some people will protest vigorously. The prosperity of that epoch is an article of faith. The writer will perhaps even be quoted against himself. Did he not write ten years ago, and has he not affirmed at every point that growing prosperity characterized not only the whole 18th century, but also the beginning of the following century? Without doubt: but the growth was very irregular. . . . The phase of economic development which extended from 1733 to 1817 was not a uniform bloc. It included, independently of the short term rises and falls, which are not in question at the moment, some periods of slow progress, some periods of accelerated progress, and exceptionally some of decline. It got under way very slowly between 1733 and 1764. It picked up speed just after the Seven Years War, became exceptionally rapid,

From C. E. Labrousse, *La crise de l'economie française à la fin de l'Ancien Régime et au début de la Révolution* (2 vols. in one, Paris, 1943), Introduction, pp. xxii–lii. Translated by the Editor. By permission Presses Universitaires de France.

and had reached its high point for the century, when the crisis of 1770 checked the surge of prosperity. After a normal cyclical readjustment – which, again, does not interest us here – there began about 1778 an abnormal decline which ended about 1787. The basic trend was then resumed and lasted, in spite of occasional crises of a very different character, into the last years of the century, extending finally into the Consular and Imperial epoch after which it accelerated even more rapidly.

We will consider for the moment only the period before 1778, only the prosperous times of moderate or rapid advance, prior to the decline which extended over most of the reign of Louis XVI. Prices had been going up since the beginning of the second third of the century. The consequences of this are well known. This long term movement dominated everything, and set the whole economy in motion. The economic order moved under its own steam. At this stage is found the traditional "18th century" which in general is fairly well known – but which remains also in general to be explained.

Agricultural production increased. Slowly, without doubt. Its inelasticity created obstacles: its inherent, permanent inelasticity . . . , but also still in the 18th century an inelasticity stemming from historic causes, temporary in character and peculiar to an economy of the old type. This rise could affect those in the business of agriculture only if they had something to sell, that is, if they had at their disposal a saleable surplus. This was the case with most of the wine-growers, and especially the big vintners of the villages. But it was the exception in the case of the producers of wheat and meat: the large-scale farm proprietor sold his produce, but not the small one, not the mass of share-croppers, nor the mass of holders of tiny parcels of land. Their situation then was quite different from what it became in the following century. Agricultural techniques, the manner of life, and the rural institutions of the time all help to explain this situation. The need for seed made a heavy drain; as much as a fifth or even a quarter of the average harvest. The yields per unit of land were small and the practice of leaving a portion of land fallow reduced by a third or one half the usable portion of any holding. But if a holding produced only a little, the mere subsistence of the holder required a great deal: all work was done by hand and to keep a pair of hands going required three pounds of bread a day.

Finally there were the deductions in kind required for the ecclesiastical tithe and the seigneurial dues. These different deductions meant that a farmer of a piece of land, who a century later was to be a seller of produce on a large scale, was in the middle of the 18th century reduced to living within a closed economy, or even, very frequently, buying food. The greatest portion of the lands of France was accordingly held by plebeian peasantry excluded from benefiting from the rise in prices. Except for the wine-grower, the favorable price situation benefited only a small minority of farmers, who alone were thereby encouraged to extend or intensify their cultivation.

This minority held, it is true, a proportion of the land relatively much greater than their number. And the tenant farmer was the more encouraged to produce in that he amply profited from the rise in prices. If the increase in rent to which he was subjected each time his leases were renewed tended to diminish the amount that he benefited from that rise in favor of the non-exploiting owner, the lessee nevertheless profited over the term of the lease, which meant, very often, over a period of nine years. A comparison of the curves of prices and rents shows clearly that the movement of prices preceded that of rents so that the former rose first. The movement of rents only followed along behind rather slowly, with a considerable time lag. Altogether, from 1730 to 1770–1775, the profit of the leasing farmer increased in three ways relative to rents which were themselves rising sharply: first during the term of the lease when prices were advancing more quickly than rents; secondly, at the time of the renewal of the lease when the new higher rent agreed upon actually took up only a portion of the actual advance; and finally over a whole succession of leases, by the increase — limited without doubt, but certain — in the quantities produced from the same land. On the other hand the rise in the price of wine enriched a great number of growers. These farm profits were accumulated and reinvested in the farming enterprise in a kind of an instinctive fashion, in this way financing the further extension of cultivation. Tenant farmers and farm owners used them to add hands, to construct new buildings, and to buy tools. There was in the last part of the period a movement toward the clearing of new land. Productive capital was increasing. It paid for an increasing number of farm hands. The class of farmer-entrepreneurs, that is to say of farmer-merchants, experienced a long period of prosperity. The rural market grew larger.

For his part, the proprietor who leased out his farm land had no reason to complain. His situation was very close to that of the actual exploiting farmer if he was paid in produce. If he was paid in money he collected rents that were rising sharply all along and which even accelerated after 1770. The possessor of seigneurial obligations payable in agricultural produce — to whom must be added the tithe-owner — seems to have had even more reason to congratulate himself on the fortunate conjunction of conditions. He gained automatically, or almost so, with respect to both prices and quantities to the extent that they both rose. His share was adjusted each year relative to the harvest. As a seller he benefited immediately from the rising prices. Therefore, the seigneurial rent income in kind, in contrast to the money rent of the bourgeois land owner, suffered no time lag in the realization of profit. At least theoretically, when these rights were not leased out — which practice was quite common, although not the general rule. Only a small part then, of the more astute seigneurial proprietors held in this respect an advantage over the bourgeois owner. Another advantage from which they benefited everywhere in common, these seigneurial proprietors and the large bourgeois proprietors who had at their disposal rents paid in kind, was that as "grain speculators" by vocation and as holders of enormous stocks, they had large quantities to sell at the high points of the rise; while at times of low prices their commodities could escape from the home market and seek out in distant markets, thanks to the freedom to export from which they principally benefited, the most remunerative price. The rise in "bourgeois" and "seigneurial" prices tended thus to exceed that of the "tenant-farmers" price. For one very important product and precisely the one which rose in price the most, the owners retained the entire benefit of the rise. Timber beat all records in its rise; and forest land, an important element of all great estates, was never rented out. The economic rent of the aristocrat in this instance was in no way diminished by peasant profits. . . .

. . . Like the rural market the urban market grew. Industrial production, flexible by nature, increased greatly, very much more quickly than agricultural production, and called for more workers. No one could consume twice as much bread, but many people could be twice as well lodged or dressed. Colonial products were at all times the greatest gainers. Starting at a very low level, they benefited from the progress of the cities where they found their principal clientele and the preference which they were given over other products. They prospered along with the sea-ports, with all the great cities, and with the increasing concentrations of population. They increased also at the expense of certain home products; the French wine-producer, for example, never recovered from the competition of coffee; although the effect came later in the last quarter of the century, not during the period under discussion.

The economic advance was thus general, covering all areas of production. There were no weak spots. Industrial profit increased more than agricultural profit or rent as the result of the success of more flexible production. Profits from colonial goods increased even more than from industry, with perhaps the exception of mining. Their progress was determined by the extension of their markets and the market in this instance doubled – in proportion to the increase of the towns and to their conquests over competing products. The rapid accumulation of wealth in the hands of the entrepreneurs permitted in turn, as did the earlier accumulation of rents, the easy financing of new businesses. Productive capital was increased.

The manufacturer and the business man were therefore, in the long run, the greatest beneficiaries of this economic advance. The commercial and industrial bourgeois class increased in numbers and power. And so did also along with them, it should not be forgotten, that whole group of landed bourgeoisie and that aristocracy of the business world which reinvested its farm rents in business. Industrial and commercial profits carried land rents along with them and accelerated and prolonged their rise.

The long term rise in agricultural prices, the *"bon prix"* of the Physiocrats, was the source of all this prosperity. It was the rise in prices which stimulated the tenant farmer and the farm owner-merchants to extend their holdings; which increased profits; which extended markets; and which opened a widening rural market – an essential element of prosperity in an "agricultural kingdom." It was this rise which increased rents, and the expenditures which made the towns grow, and financed and stimulated at the same time an industrial production which was doubly encouraged by the extension of both urban and rural markets. And it was the prosperity of the towns which produced in turn the prosperity of the trade in colonial products.

All was then for the best, it seemed, in the economic state. At least for the active citizens, for those who had at their disposal a significant quantity of productive capital, which is to say, entrepreneurs and persons of means. But there were also the passive citizens, the mass of wage earners of both city and country. A group with little homogeneity, no doubt, but of immense size and made up of some permanent wage earners, proletarians in the strict sense, and some occasional wage workers such as small land owners, share-croppers and small tenant farmers. All these gained in their own way from the economic trend, although they had no produce to sell.

A hundred years ago some "optimistic" juggler of facts might perhaps have written that they gained most. They did indeed gain in life expectancy. The 18th century – the whole 18th century, both before and after 1778 – was marked by a revolution in mortality rates. The birth rate remained constant, or very near. But something new appeared, something important, on the curve of the death rate. There no longer appeared in the population curve as had been true in the preceding century and was still true even in 1709, those enormous troughs at those points of most acute economic crises. . . . The population was no longer submitted to those periodic decimations which never permitted it to rise above a certain level. From the 14th to the beginning of the 18th century, it seems to have oscillated at around twenty millions in spite of a high birth rate resulting normally in a surplus of births, but from time to time an enormous rise in the price of grain would suddenly halt the whole economic mechanism – to think only of crises in the supply of food is to see only one side of things – and this would result in a loss of the surplus population built up by the normal excess of births over deaths. The mortality would naturally be the greatest among the lower classes: share-croppers, day laborers, and wage earners of town and country would bear the brunt of these heavy massacres. Nothing like this happened during the whole period which is our concern. The periodic fluctuations in the economy diminished. The price curve no longer rose over a very brief span to three times its former level, but only occasionally doubled, and often very much less than that. It no longer carved out underneath it those tremendous troughs in the population curve. The economic crises doubtless continued to be very serious. They left some dead and wounded on the field, but nothing like the human sacrifices of the earlier period. Almost stable for several centuries, the population suddenly began to rise. The population increase received its impetus from the natural increase of the proletariat, since the latter survived the crises in larger numbers. Its natural increase surpassed that of all other classes. It was the chief beneficiary of that revolution in the mortality rate. Not that its standard of living had generally risen, nor was the long term trend of "real" wages on the rise; quite the contrary, as will be seen in a moment. But the periodic disasters had lost their virulence. Their amplitude had fallen a notch. These crises killed very many fewer of the day laborers, workers, share-croppers and small holders. As a consequence a proletariat, or quasi-proletariat without employment, rapidly surfeited the labor market. It had without doubt at least avoided condemnation to death in that it was no longer devoured uselessly, and gluttonously in great masses. It seemed that a foresighted Nature was allowing them to accumulate and thus provide employers with an immense labor reserve. And so allowed to live, the wage-earner paid for that concession with forced labor at the lowest rates. . . .

There is no doubt that the demographic revolution of the 18th century considerably worsened the workers' already relatively bad position, by the sudden increase in workers available. Elsewhere it had that result. If the wage curve finally reacted and turned upward it was well after that of prices and with less strength.

Productive capital increased, however, day by day, under the stimulus of the rise in prices and profits. Building, textiles, urban trade; there was not a single profession where the volume of business did not rise. The whole "flexible" area of production furthered in large measure the population thrust. But that area was not yet very extended. This flexible segment of the economy was still only secondary. There was needed a market of another kind to absorb the sudden population increase which arose from all of peasant France. Doubtless agricultural production required more workers too, fortunately. The grape-grower with his great need for hands used an increasing number of wage laborers and share-croppers. The land planted in grain required more cultivators, more day laborers, and more threshers: prices were increasing faster than rents and a rise in profits was in full swing. But advances in production, as has already been noted, were still made very slowly. With its great dependence on hand labor, agricultural production with its traditional inelasticity stood in striking contrast to the sudden elasticity of the population.

In summary, then, it can be said that the progress in the formation of productive capital permitted the absorption of increasing quantities of labor, but insufficient quantities considering the violence of the population increase. The number of workers employed increased. Wage rates increased. The total amount paid out in wages was accordingly increased by these two means. It was not merely a nominal but a "real" gain. That total volume of wages could buy, in total, in spite of the rise in prices, more bread, more meat, more textiles and more colonial products. It increased in money terms by perhaps three quarters while the cost of living rose by only one half. The wage fund increased in absolute value and in purchasing power. But the human divisor increased even more rapidly. In the end the "real" share of each individual diminished. This fall in wages stands in contrast to the increase in the return on capital during this period.

This was, however, only a minor ill. So long as profits held up all went well. In the world of entrepreneurs and property owners, an optimistic wind prevailed. Business was spectacularly good and easily obtained. If the condition of the worker declined in an absolute sense, the opportunities for work at least were increasing. How could one fail to be satisfied? The economic system was performing its function satisfactorily. It was, after all, up to the birth rate to be reasonable.

This situation as outlined, at first barely evident, then more clearly so, and then finally affirmed most strongly, was characteristic of the whole 18th century, from the beginning of the long term rise in prices up until the cyclical crisis of 1770.

But after the flare-up of prosperity which took place just after the Seven Years War, and after the exceptional advance of 1763–1770 which marked the height of economic prosperity under the Old Regime, the situation was reversed. With the coming of that unfortunate monarch, Louis XVI, the winds changed. Not all of them, doubtless, and not all at the same time. Some of them still blew, but weakly; while others died away. But the most important of them began to blow in the opposite direction. The economic weather changed for the worse. A period of economic distress, a period of contraction, set in.

The initial date of the downswing, or a clear point of demarcation, from the preceding period is rather difficult to mark off, since the reversal did not set in everywhere at the same time or in the same fashion. But by the end of 1778 at the latest, it was an accomplished fact. Prices were everywhere in full decline.

Those of wine fell in a short time by half: that had happened by 1781 and they remained at this level for a long period of seven years. The collapse of profits in the wine industry, an important category of profit for the small farmer in the country, struck a considerable number of producers and even the great proprietors did not escape disaster in the fine wine trade as well as in the ordinary grades. The price of grains fell also between 1770 and 1780, and then remained relatively low until 1787. The fall, however, did not become serious until the end of 1776, and the amount of the decline was nowhere near as great as that of wine. It hit particularly hard on the great grain producing areas, that area of tenant farms which covered a vast portion of the northern half of France, extending from Lorraine to Normandy and from Flanders to Orleans. Doubtless it did not affect the profits of the small holder as much as the fall in wine prices had earlier. But all the different categories of farmer-merchants who had profited formerly in good times, suffered now from the reversal of economic forces. The farmer who owned his land and the tenant farmer were no longer stimulated to extend their cultivated areas.

The situation of the tenant farmer became especially difficult since his profit was pinched between the fall in his return from sales and the advance in rents. Up to about 1770–1775, the movement of rents lagged behind the increase in gross income. The renter when making his agreement accepted an increase in rent, more or less based on the level of the current price at the date of the renewal of the contract, and in the end he had found it to be a good bargain since prices continued to rise during the nine year term of the lease. With the falling off in the price of grains, the situation was reversed. The lessee who had made an agreement in the period 1770–1775 based on the high prices then current found he was losing instead of gaining because prices fell during the course of the period of his lease. But it was thought that it was a temporary situation and it did not dampen the enthusiasm of prospective renters who remained optimistic because of the earlier rise which had lasted for a generation. The decline and the lower prices were not taken seriously. The owner, for his part, had a chance to get revenge. Up until that point he had not paid much attention to the rise. For too long a time he had allowed the renter to put one over on him. He had not foreseen in time the unprecedented rise of 1763–1770 and in consequence he had not received his full return. The situation had taken him by surprise; he had been tricked and did not intend to be a second time. It was the moment for rent to boldly recoup what it had lost by its earlier lagging behind. The more so because prospective renters were not lacking nor was money. The population rise had increased the number of prospective tenants and had swelled the ranks of the peasant family. Heads of families waited with their full complement of children at the door of the farm. And the gains of better times had not yet been spent. Either they were held in hard cash, or they had been used to buy small parcels of land which the tenant farmer sub-let, like a *rentier,* at a high rent, of course, to those less fortunate than he. He would still willingly accept a renewal of his lease on less favorable terms. Prices continued to fall and although the decline certainly eventually stopped, they stayed relatively low until 1787. So great was the demand for leases that on the whole rents rose at a very lively rate during the last fifteen or twenty years of the monarchy — very much more quickly than in 1760 to 1770 and against the general economic trend. After having worked against the lessor, the economic situation then turned against the lessee — which is to say, in most cases, against the peasant who in this way had to make restitution to the proprietor of more than he had taken from him earlier.

The crisis first struck the wine-industry, then the wheat market, and finally developed into a general crisis of agricultural profits. One can see the repercussions which it had on employment and on the condition of the working class. Instead of increasing as it had during the preceding period, productive capital tended to decrease, and with it naturally the demand for workers. . . .

Industry as a whole languished. The figures on the volume of trade are also explicit: foreign sales fell off. Only the colonial market remained on the increase.

Colonial trade: how many optimistic miscalculations have been caused by it! Open at random any work or any chapter on the economic state of France during the reign of Louis XVI. The documentary proofs offered are the statistics of Arnould on foreign commerce which make evident an immense increase in that trade over the whole century. From them it has been concluded that there was an increase of the same order continued right through the period of Louis XVI. And to infer from the advance in foreign trade an equivalent development in interior trade, thereby furnishing an index of industrial production, was only a step and one which was generally taken without hesitation. The approximations and errors of Arnould we will return to in good time. But while the trend which is discernible from these tables is accurate for the overall picture, it is, however, necessary to analyze the figures, by going back to the author's sources themselves to the accounts or registers of the balance of trade, and thereby to reconstitute on an annual basis the graph of our international trade. It is also necessary to distinguish between commerce carried on with the colonies and that with other countries, and better yet, the trade in colonial products as compared with domestic products. When this procedure is used it appears that after a great rise extending over the first two thirds of the century, there was a certain stagnation of French exports beginning a dozen years before the American War, and which these hostilities actually converted into a decline. The level of this stagnant period seems to have been surpassed in 1785 but then only slightly, and definite progress was resumed only in 1786–1787, at the very time when the long intercyclical depression was about to be dissipated.

Up until the end of the reign of Louis XVI the last third of the 18th century stands in contrast on this point to the first two thirds. The curve of exports also marks in its own way a break in the trend. If there was not an actual decline, and if even the leveling off segment of the curve went up slightly, there is no longer found here the same vigor as in the preceding period. But the leveling off segment was only kept from actually showing a decline thanks to the enormous rise in the colonial figures. That is, the figures for exports from the mother country to the colonies, and, most important, the rise shown in the re-exportation of colonial products. It was not wheat, or wine — in spite of the increase in the export of brandy — nor cloth, nor linen goods, nor the young cotton industry which made the fortune of our flag, but rather sugar and coffee. The ambiguous figures for our commercial statistics accordingly do not afford the certain proofs which they are often called on to supply. They no longer have the broad significance for France which has been attributed to them. A rapidly increasing exportation of important national commodities produced in national shops or factories with French labor, would doubtless have constituted a symptom of national prosperity. A resale of colonial products which were only slightly altered at home signifies infinitely less. The re-export of more sugar doubtless meant that more sugar had been produced in the Islands, that the merchant marine was busy, that the shipyards were active and that business was good at Bordeaux and Nantes. But the economic impact of this trade was not proportional to its statistical weight — to the large place that it occupied in the figures for foreign trade. The rise in the resale of sugar is for us only an accessory index. It signifies that the magnates of San Domingo were accumulating legendary fortunes and were buying hoards of Negro slaves, but it does not signify that French profits were going up or that French unemployment was reduced.

And unemployment was then indeed the great affliction of both town and country. The misfortunes of the wine-grower, of the farmer and manufacturer, and the stabilization or decline of agricultural and industrial production obviously had the effect of reducing the overall demand for workers. And even though the rates of money wages may have resisted the trend and real wages held up, the total number of employed persons went down. And real wages did not increase in spite of the sharp drop in prices of wine and the lesser ones in grains because retail prices fell much less than wholesale and the prices of other articles like meat, wood, rents, colonial products and even clothing because of the effect of the shortage of raw materials, actually went up. The economy ceased for a time to advance, to expand, and prices obtained for commodities no longer included any profit. The tempo of production slowed down at the same time when the rate of production per man was going up and the population still continued to increase as in the preceding period both freely and naturally after the manner of compound interest. The proletariat swelled in numbers not only from natural increase but also by the movement into its ranks by men from other classes such as discouraged small owners or "disappointed" tenant farmers. Unemployment increased. The old problem of mouths and the food to fill them, already aggravated during the first two thirds of the century by the decline in the mortality rate, entered an acute stage and for a time became much more explicit as the conflict implicit between a revolutionary increase in population and an economy in a state of contraction became most strikingly apparent.

. . . It is evident that as seen from a distance and in perspective, the recession of the 70's seems to have been only an incident, quite quickly overcome. It seemed longer to contemporaries. And the typical cyclical crisis which developed in 1789 after an intervening spell of recovery lasting for a year or two, fell upon an economy in a low state of resistance.

Following the moderately long pre-Revolutionary recession, the year 1787 saw the beginning of the Revolutionary cyclical downswing which was dominated by the crisis of 1789 and which covered a period of five years, ending in 1791.

A serious accident of a kind that happened periodically occurred in 1788. The grain harvest was very bad and in an economy of the old type this usually foreshadowed an imminent and general crisis. The harvest of the year following was still only mediocre. However, at other times, the situation had been worse. The 1788 drop came after a whole series of years with surpluses and 1787 had been among the best. If prices moved violently and attained previously unequaled figures, if the previous peak reached in 1770 was surpassed in 1789, and if a plateau of high prices persisted from mid-1789 to mid-1790, nevertheless the rise reached only 50% above the cyclical minimum of 1786. This is without question a very considerable proportion but it was still very much lower than that of many other periods of crisis. The spread had amounted to 100% twenty years earlier in 1770, and it was again 100% twenty years later in 1812, and again in 1817. The rise of 1789–1790, although sudden, sharp and very much blamed for causing all the economic difficulties even though it carried prices to a new level, did not set a new record, or anywhere near it with respect to the amplitude of the spread between its high and low points. But it did strike an economy which was just recovering and still upset from a serious and persistent economic *malaise,* as well as from the shock of 1785. And the political shock of 1789 in turn complicated the crisis since it disquieted the manufacturer and business man, seriously disturbed the luxury trade, and caused the flight of both men and capital.

The character of this periodic crisis became apparent in the second half of 1788. The bad harvest as usual determined everything that followed. In the first place, so far as the country regions were concerned, where the farmer-merchant had only too little to sell, the small quantities at his disposal prevented him from profiting from the rise in price. The price only served as an enticement, moreover, when he brought his harvest to market in late September or November. Nor did the high prices of 1789 generally benefit him. His revenue declined. The price of meat was low, but urban consumption was reduced, and so at another point the income of the farmer declined. The vintner, at first glance seemed to be less badly off. The grape harvest of 1788 was unquestionably mediocre but prices were very much higher. Profit from the harvest year 1788–1789 declined very little. But the wine-grower was, however, a purchaser of bread and although he held his own, or very nearly, as a producer, he found his position as a consumer very much worsened in 1789 because of the drastic seasonal rise in prices. The crisis thus struck all the important sectors of agricultural production, the farmer-merchant, as well as the operators of farming enterprises that had rather extended themselves in order to have at their disposal a saleable surplus. Both of these were relatively worse off in spite of high prices after having deducted the necessary amounts to feed their families, to pay their dues in kind, and in the case of the grain grower, the amount needed for seed. The situation of the vast peasant proletariat was even worse. The seller of his labor appears to have been even more unfavorably situated than the seller of wheat, meat, or wine. Periodic unemployment increased while production decreased. There was less wheat to be harvested and, above all, less wheat to be threshed, as well as fewer grapes to be gathered.

On the other hand the price of grain did not stop rising. As between the seasonal low of 1788 and the high of 1789, the rise amounted to two thirds over the whole country. As usual the most popular grains rose even more – rye rose as much as three fourths. This amounts to saying that all the income of the day laborer had to go for his sustenance in the most literal sense and that he deferred all purchases that could be put off and especially those of textiles. The farmer-merchant, whose position has been indicated, did the same. The rural market for goods was closed off.

One can guess what happened with respect to manufacturing and building. Deprived of its agricultural clientele, textiles weakened. The manufacturer knew only too well by the second half of 1788 the fate which the prevailing conditions had in store for him. He knew these situations. The rise in the price of bread would affect the artisan and the wage worker of the towns no less than the producer and day laborer of the country, and like the rural clientele and for the same reasons urban consumers were going to be lacking. Profits fell. Industrial unemployment grew worse. In the last quarter of 1788 the gravity of the situation surpassed all expectations. The national production of cloth collapsed. In 1789 it amounted to no more than half of the figure for 1787. Unemployment became a catastrophe, employment falling like production at least 50%. Wage rates themselves fell, being more flexible in industry than in agriculture. Building, for its part, languished as a result of both the agricultural and industrial crisis which had reduced the available funds of the landed proprietors as well as causing the insolvency of other buyers whether they were employers or wage earners. Perhaps in the long run the depression in the towns exceeded that in the rural areas. Already undermined for more than ten years by the decline in profits and widespread unemployment, the whole economy crumbled under the shock of 1789. One must accept the fact that in the *cahiers* one is seeing something more than the typical whining of voters or taxpayers. The compilers of the *cahiers* did not exaggerate; it was the crisis which exaggerated all the usual ills. . . .

From the foregoing the Revolution indeed appears in many respects as it did to Michelet, and in contradiction to the ideas of Jaurès as later taken up by Mathiez, to have been a revolution stemming from misery. Not that Jaurès and Mathiez denied the reality and the influence of misery, but according to them it played only a minor and incidental role. That might have been the case if the economic crisis of 1789 had been only what it seems at first glance, namely, a simple crisis caused by a shortage of food supplies resulting from the devastating hailstorms of 1788 which could be quickly, or fairly quickly relieved, by favorable weather and the relief efforts undertaken by the new National Assembly. . . . In this view, distress was the result of a kind of meteorological disaster. The economic breakdown of 1788–1790 was unfortunately of another character. It struck the whole French economy; from grain and wine to textiles and building construction — an economy already sorely strained by economic difficulties from which it had just barely begun to escape and especially the severe forage crisis of 1785. Without doubt the sharp cyclical downswing of the French economy in 1789, and along with it, as has also been suspected, the pre-Revolutionary depression, did produce the economic circumstances which were the occasion for the Revolution, but this situation was responsible to a very much greater degree than Jaurès and Mathiez realized. Both of these factors profoundly affected the events of 1789 and 1790. They were no less influential ultimately in their effect on social and economic institutions, although prior to 1789 they had produced no durable changes in the most important laws relating to the social and fiscal order. In this way then they are causes.

The Revolution was born in the midst of a government financial crisis which was itself the result of the debt contracted to carry on the American War of 1777–1783. According to some, one could put it even more strongly — that without the American War there would have been no financial crisis of the government, no convocation of the Estates General and no Revolution — at least at the time and in the form in which it actually broke out. The Revolution considered as an event, therefore, stems from a political fact. But it also proceeded from an economic fact with financial consequences, namely the recession. Without the war, there would have been no American debt, no massive increase in governmental expenses, no initial difficulty:

but with the recession, there were no resources, no possible increase in tax receipts, no remedies for the critical situation – or rather no resources and only remedies that would have been very difficult to apply. It had been necessary for the government to put out of consideration any increase in the major consumption taxes since the excess levy of 1781. The amount of income from the *taille* had remained fixed since 1780. A second *vingtième* had been imposed in 1782 and was to expire in 1787. The small spontaneous rise in the consumption taxes was not sufficient to be of any importance. The income from the excise taxes certainly increased with the substitution of the direct administration of the excise taxes for the tax farm, and with the rapid increase in population, and the ever more rapid growth of the cities which were great consumers of wine and spirits, and with the ever increasing extension of an exchange economy. The peasant masses who emigrated to the towns paid a tax on the wine they drank at the cafe whereas before they were free of any tax on the wine produced from their own vines in a closed economy situation. The crisis in viniculture itself helped to raise the income from the excise taxes by obliging the wine producer to convert the wine which he was not able to sell to brandy which was more heavily taxed proportionately. The consumption taxes accordingly held up against the trend of the economy or even increased a little. But the return from them would have been far greater in an expanding economy with the characteristic rising price scale which would have automatically increased gross incomes in proportion to the price rise which would in turn have stimulated the peasant to plant more and so would have increased the total quantity of taxable commodities. On the other hand with a rise in profits it would have been possible to increase the surtax and even increase the amount of the *taille*.

It is assuredly an unusual occupation for the historian to concern himself with what might have happened in history rather than what actually did take place. But let's assume hypothetically that in the period of the American War and the years immediately following, there had occurred the same conjunction of economic forces as prevailed at the beginning of the following century; that is to say, a rapidly expanding economy. Is it going too far to say that it would have been easier for the government to make up the deficit? Or, at least, that increasing government revenues would have constituted a very satisfactory security for the loans which might have had to have been floated? The controller general would not have had to overcome at the same time the costs of the American War and the evasions of the French taxpayer. He could have deferred the convocation of the Assembly of Notables and postponed his appeal to the privileged classes, which is to say, to that group which was in fact the chief beneficiary of the long term rise in rents. It was land rents which during the century had constituted the single most important category of increasing income and was the one on which the privileged classes refused with the greatest obstinacy to be taxed. Under those hypothetical circumstances the Old Regime would not have been imperatively compelled to carry out a fiscal revolution of such a kind that in fact it amounted to a renunciation of its own basic principles nor, on the other hand, would it have had to convoke the nation to make that revolution for it.

Accordingly the financial consequences of that long pre-Revolutionary recession and the Revolutionary economic crisis were grave. They prevented, or at least hindered the adjustment of receipts to expenses. The income of the state continued to be insufficient. But as a result of the recession and the crisis even that amount which the taxpayer was already paying became too heavy a burden. The tax rate was not reduced – far from it. But even if it had remained almost fixed since 1782, it should not be forgotten that it was raised in that year, just as it had been in the preceding one – although these increases were moderate. It was not so much that the rate of taxation had increased as that the taxpayers' ability to pay had diminished. The fall in prices had produced a decline in business activity which was accompanied by a disproportionately heavy fall in profit; so although the tax rate remained theoretically the same, in the face of declining profits it very soon assumed monstrous proportions. This "fiscal reaction" was felt throughout the nation and automatically the masses of the nation arrayed themselves against it.

This little known "fiscal reaction" had as its counterpart a "seigneurial reaction" which is very much better known. A seigneurial reaction, the origins of which can also be seen in the economic distress which dominated the whole reign of Louis XVI. The seigneurial proprietor was seeking an increase in the number of payments in kind in order to compensate for the decreasing value of the existing payments which naturally followed from the decline in prices. This was especially true of the men who leased from the seigneur the right to collect these payments, as was without doubt the most frequent situation, and who took this means of defending themselves against the fall in prices when, confident of a rise, they had contracted for renewals of their leases at a higher figure. Like the royal taxes, the seigneurial levies increased immeasurably in proportion to profits which fell drastically; at least on the lands subjected to some types of seigneurial levy, such as those held on *champart,* for example.

But besides this "seigneurial reaction," as it is generally understood, which perhaps fell on only a small proportion of the lands, there was another seigneurial reaction which struck all tenants automatically and universally whether they paid *champart* or the ecclesiastical *dîme,* the latter being in this respect similar to seigneurial rights. This was the increased burden borne by all who paid any kind of a levy in kind proportional to his gross product. In a situation of falling prices, profit which derives from net product falls proportionately more than gross income or gross product, with the result that any payments that had to be made in a fixed proportion to gross product were necessarily transformed in times of recession or economic crisis into a progressive tax on net product. Accordingly in the decade before the Revolution anyone subject to this kind of an obligation was, in effect, subjected to an additional charge even though the rate remained the same.

This universal and prolonged fiscal reaction and the comparable seigneurial reaction accordingly arrayed against the royal fisc and the complex of feudal obligations the whole mass of people on whom these weighed so heavily, not only just during the great economic crisis of 1789 when the reactions reached their peak but also during the whole decade preceding it. The proletariat was no better off. The day laborer who was employed fewer days and who was raising a larger family, also paid a tax at first increasing, and then constant—which meant progressive in both instances—on an income which was declining. If he held a plot of land as either owner or renter, which was very often the case, then he suffered equally on his mixed income from the increasing pressure of seigneurial rights which reached its maximum at the time of the crisis of 1789.

As for royal taxes, it sufficed simply for them to remain constant to become a more formidable burden. Open the *cahiers!* Look in them for an explanation of the crisis! It is always the royal taxes which are the guilty parties. It was the taxes which discouraged cultivation, which were crushing the share-cropper and the farmer. It was the excise taxes which were ruining the wine-industry by causing a collapse in the market and devouring the profit. Those private taxes, the seigneurial rights, produced some analagous complaints. The same complaints at all times? Perhaps. Were these absurd complaints to the extent that they blamed royal taxes for the crisis? Surely. But, nevertheless, they were sincere complaints, and complaints well founded to the extent that they blamed the prevailing disproportion between profits and taxes, between wages and taxes. To this provocative increase of royal and seigneurial levies they presently reacted with more than just complaints. The offices of the tax collector and the customs officers were put to the torch. They marched out to reclaim the grain collected as a feudal levy which was lying in the seigneurs' barns. From the well-to-do leaseholding farmer to the agricultural day laborer, a whole people were in agreement, drawn together by the universal decline in farm income; by their common antagonism to the fiscal and seigneurial reaction. The towns joined the chorus against the excise taxes on consumption goods, and against the seigneur as a manipulator in the grain market using the grain he collected as rent. There resulted from this not only episodes and events like those seen in the peasant uprisings of 1789 and 1790 but also some relatively permanent laws like those which suppressed the excise taxes and the salt tax and which transformed and lightened the levy on consumption goods. This situation also produced some definitive and permanent laws like those which suppressed the ecclesiastical *dîme* and abolished all feudal obligations.

The consequences of pre-Revolutionary economic distress for both fiscal and general economic policy constituted in themselves a revolution. Not, without doubt, the whole Revolution. But one can, however, even argue that the consequences of these economic difficulties were even more far reaching because men of the younger generation, meaning all those less than thirty years of age in 1789, who had never known anything since their entry into economic life except declining profits and a shortage of work, tended to blame their troubles on the Old Regime itself. Their elders, who had lost part of the profits accumulated in better times or who had continued to suffer a decline in wages, had the same attitude. But such reactions are not to be found only in that period. One finds them both earlier and later. It matters little that a free economy is by definition an uncontrolled economy; when economic distress arises contemporaries always blame the government. The fact that royal taxes in this instance were blamed for the crisis has already been indicated. Taxes are a political institution and starting with the *taille* and the excise taxes, criticism led inevitably from them to the controller, then to the ministry, and finally to the regime itself. But taxes alone, one can be sure, did not appear to the subjects as the only thing to be blamed. From all sides there arose a discordant clamor of accusations to the effect that if there were recessions and cyclical economic crises, it was not only because the tax burden was excessive, but also because government expenses themselves were excessive. The deficit and the collapse of the government's credit, far from being consequences, seemed to contemporaries to be causes; causes of the general uncertainty, of the timidity of capital, of the ruin of the spirit of enterprise. Why did this long period of economic contraction, this long period of falling or unstable prices for grains, this long decline in the wine market take place? Because the government had mistakenly prohibited exportation. Because too much had been produced. The government could have imposed restrictions but did not do so. Why did it not revive the prohibitions against planting new vines? Why this rapid and furious rise in the prices of grain in 1789? Although it was conceded that doubtless the bad harvest was somewhat responsible for this situation, still the people accused the speculators and the government which had allowed too much wheat to be exported in 1787 and did not import enough in 1788. Marat denounced Necker by name as a speculator. If agriculture lacked capital, it was not because the profit of the cultivator was declining, but because of the fiscal inequalities, and because of the exemptions and privileges conferred on the towns because their financial prospects were more highly regarded. The economic evils then were of political origin.

The remedy proposed was political also, "a system of regulation" more liberal in character would suffice. If industry languished, like agriculture, it was necessary to blame the foreign customs barriers unless, of course, it was the lack of protection of the French market. It was neither the crucial shortage of forage in 1785, nor the rising price of wool, nor the rising price of cotton, nor the general decline in incomes which was the cause of industrial distress, but the Anglo-French treaty of commerce. And if population increased at a dangerous rate it was the fault of the military system of the government, since the militia system encouraged marriage and penalized celibacy. All classes launched a volley of accusations against the regime, and it can be seen that certain of these were well founded, and that many of the factors seized upon by public opinion as "causes" of the discomfort or misery indeed had an influence as contributory factors on the long protracted crisis of the French economy. But those which were in fact only accessory, the public thought of as the crucial factors. In this way there arose and thickened the atmosphere of discontent in which the Revolution broke out. Thus a grievous error in the placing of blame made a political crisis grow out of the economic crisis.

Thus, the revolutionary events themselves, as well as some of the important economic policies and institutions which emerged from the Revolution, had their origin in large part in the decline in profits and wages, in the straitened circumstances of the industrialist, the artisan, the tenant farmer, the small owner, and the distress of the wage earner and the day laborer. An unfavorable concatenation of events brought together in a common opposition the bourgeoisie and the proletariat. From this viewpoint the Revolution appears to a much greater degree than Jaurès and Mathiez have allowed, as a revolution arising out of misery. . . .

THE FRENCH REVOLUTION AND THE PEASANTS

GEORGES LEFEBVRE

Now emeritus professor of French Revolutionary history of the University of Paris, M. Lefebvre continues to carry on active research and publication on that subject. In addition to his pioneering work on the social and economic aspects of the Revolution, he has also published several general studies of the era which are considered by scholars to be the best and most authoritative works on the period now available. Although an admirer of Mathiez and his work, he has remained free of the latter's rather narrow materialist preconceptions and has consistently held a moderate republican viewpoint. The following selection is a portion of two lectures given at the Sorbonne in 1932 and later published in one of the scholarly journals devoted to the history of the Revolution.

IT IS not my purpose to retrace even in broad outline the role of the peasants in the events of the Revolution, nor to describe the conditions under which they lived during the last years of the Old Regime and up to the beginning of the nineteenth century. What I am concerned with here is to show that it is necessary to recognize that the peasants hold an important place in the history of the Revolution and thereby not only to extend our knowledge of that event, but also to integrate it more exactly into the historical perspective of the French nation, and by this same means to shed further light on the basic character of our civilization. This is not the first occasion which has been offered me to present the conclusions to which my research and reflections have led me. But having noted that Mathiez himself has not accorded to the peasants the attention which in my opinion they merit, it has seemed to me not inappropriate that I should present the reasons for my opinion in more detail. . . .

I

The French Revolution has for a long time been presented as the work of the *philosophes,* and in the books of Aulard it still appears essentially as an ideological fact. It was Jaurès who accustomed historians to look on it as a sociological fact and consequently of economic origin. This does not mean, of course, that the ideas of the *philosophes* must be denied any importance whatsoever and are to be looked upon only as a symptom and not a cause. Between the social or economic fact and the historic event it is necessary for the mind of man to intervene if the first is to lead to the second. It is none the less true that the Revolution was only the culmination of a long social and economic development which has made the bourgeoisie masters of the world.

From Georges Lefebvre, *Etudes sur la Revolution française* (Paris, 1954), pp. 246–263. Translated by the Editor. By permission Presses Universitaires de France.

This was not a new discovery on the part of Jaurès. In the first decades of the nineteenth century, Guizot, having called upon history to support the philosophy of Royer-Collard in order to establish the Charter of 1814 on an indestructible foundation, showed in most admirable fashion how the originality of western civilization lay especially in its creation of a strong middle class, the bourgeoisie. A class which had little by little created the framework and elaborated the ideolgy of a new society, the full flowering of which was achieved by the Revolution of 1789. Tocqueville and even Taine shared this opinion. These historians, in truth, without being in any way ignorant of the fact that the origin and progress of the bourgeoisie was the result of the appearance and accumulation of mobile wealth, nevertheless were scarcely interested in the economic origins of the social movement. But Barnave even earlier, just as Jaurès reiterated it strongly later, had brought it clearly to light and the Utopian Socialists never ceased to emphasize it. Finally, in the *Communist Manifesto* of 1847, and then in the first volume of *Das Capital* in 1867, Karl Marx reaped the fruits of the slow development of that idea and by adding to it his observations on contemporary England, ended by formulating with extraordinary power the economic interpretation of history.

It must be acknowledged, however, that the historians of the Revolution have not retained very much of the Marxian formulation of the theory. It is really Jaurès who has been our teacher and he is the more worthy of that honor in that in restoring to history its social and economic base, he corrected the extremes of self-styled Marxism by maintaining very vigorously that ideas have none the less their own proper function, that they play an essential role in history, that the ruling class is not exclusively dominated by its own selfish preoccupations, and that it was sincere in its conviction that the general good of society depended upon the maintenance of its predominance.

As Jaurès presented it, however, the upheaval of 1789 appeared as a single and simple event. The Revolution was brought about by the power of a bourgeois class which had reached maturity and consequently wished to achieve legal recognition of that fact. This view seems to us today to be too summary. First, it does not explain why the accession of the bourgeoisie took place at that moment rather than at any other, nor why in France it took the form of a violent change, while it might have happened, as it did elsewhere in fact, as the result of a progressive evolution—even if not entirely peaceful. We now are well aware that the Revolution of 1789 came to pass only as the result of a truly extraordinary and unforeseen coincidence of a whole series of immediate causes; a financial crisis of exceptional gravity stemming from participation in the war of the American colonies; a crisis of unemployment engendered by the treaty of commerce of 1786 with England and war in eastern Europe; and finally a crisis of rising prices and misery provoked by the bad harvest of 1788 and by the edict of 1787 which by authorizing the export of grain had emptied the storehouses. But these are not all the factors, and the underlying causes of the Revolution seem to us also to become more and more complex. . . .

One can see that the economic interpretation of history does not succeed at all in achieving for us a simplified view of the past. The mere rise of a revolutionary class is not necessarily the sole cause of its victory and it is not inevitable that this victory take place, or in any case that it take place through violent means. In this instance the Revolution was unleashed by those whom it was to destroy, not by those who profited from it, and it cannot be proved that it was inevitable that this group should have been able to impose its will on the sovereign. It cannot be said that stronger kings might not have succeeded in limiting the progress to power of the aristocracy in the eighteenth century; nor that in 1787 and even in 1789 a greater king with more prestige would not have been able to make them listen to reason.

What is important at this moment, however, is to affirm that the Revolution was a complex event; that there was not one Revolution but several. For it does not even suffice simply to distinguish between first a revolution of the aristocracy and then one of the Third Estate. Jaurès first and Mathiez after him have rightly insisted on the rapid disintegration of the latter group and on the antagonism which promptly manifested itself between the upper bourgeoisie, the artisans and the proletariat. . . . [As a result] Mathiez . . . has been led to distinguish a third Revolution, that of August 10, 1792, which was democratic and republican in character, and then a fourth of June 2, 1793 which aimed at the establishment of a social democracy. If Babeuf had succeeded there would have been a fifth.

So be it, but the picture in my opinion is still not absolutely complete or accurate because the peasants, so to speak, have not taken their place in it. Let there not be attributed to me, for all that, the pretention of having discovered them! No historian, naturally, has been unaware of the uprisings in the rural areas nor the agrarian reforms of the Revolution. But they have been accustomed to see in the actions of the peasantry simply a repercussion of the revolt of the townsman and especially that which took place on July 14; as if the rural classes had simply obeyed the call of the bourgeoisie. They have thought of the peasants' action as directed exclusively against feudal obligations and royal authority, being thereby in full and perfect accord with the bourgeoisie — which is to say implicitly that the abolition of feudal obligations and the sale of the nationalized lands of the church as it was finally carried out gave entire satisfaction to the inhabitants of the rural villages. These are all conclusions which tend to conserve for the Revolution a majestic and homogeneous appearance — to see it only as the Revolution of the Third Estate. Even if they describe the disintegration of the latter, they appear to believe that it took place under the same conditions and produced the same results in the country as in the towns, the well-to-do peasant making common cause with the bourgeoisie and the agricultural day laborer with the town-dwelling artisan. From this point of view social programs would have been posed in the same way for one as for the other and, for example, the application of the famous Ventôse decrees would have had the same implications for the sans-culotte of the rural village as for the sans-culotte of the town.

I am not unaware, of course, that there is in all this a certain amount of truth: the example of the town did exert a profound influence on the village. There would probably not have been any French Revolution if hate for the feudal regime had not united peasant and bourgeois, and its destruction was one of the most important and most indestructible of its reforms. Finally, in both town and village social distinctions remained very similar and the classes in each did not diverge completely in interests and viewpoint. To put it briefly, the peasant revolution developed within the framework of the French Revolution.

But it is important to point out, and I am striving to do it, that there was, however, a true peasant revolution which had an autonomy of its own in its origins, development, its crises and its tendencies.

It was autonomous in its origin because the peasant masses stirred spontaneously under the influence of poverty and the hopes to which the convocation of the Estates General had given rise. Furthermore they must have at the same time as their fellow townsman, arrived at the conclusion that there was, in the summer of 1789, an aristocratic conspiracy because without that having happened, the "Great Fear" which swept over France at that time would be inexplicable. It was autonomous also in its actions and in the course it followed because up until the 14th of July the bourgeoisie had had neither the time nor was it disposed to attack the clerical tithe nor the feudal obligations. But the peasants began, as early as the month of March, to rise against their seigneurs and to refuse to pay their seigneurial dues well before the capture of the Bastille. On receipt of the news of the events in Paris, they revolted spontaneously, taking their cause into their own hands – to the great discomfiture of the bourgeoisie who in several places took it upon themselves to suppress the risings. Autonomous also it was in that it had its own crises, because agrarian revolts broke out again in 1793 under conditions that bore no necessary relation to the political development of the Revolution. Furthermore, it was even autonomous in its results, since, without the peasant revolution having taken place, one can be sure that the Constituent Assembly would have not struck such serious blows against the feudal regime, and it is not certain that it would have been finally abolished without indemnity. But that it was, above all, autonomous in its anti-capitalist tendencies, on that I would insist particularly. . . .

II

In 1789 the French peasants already held a significant portion of the soil of France; perhaps 30 to 40% on the average, sometimes very much less, sometimes very much more. That is why in comparing them to the serfs of central and eastern Europe who were forced to render uncompensated labor to their lords and to the English agricultural laborers who were free but who were reduced to living on their wages alone, one can describe the French peasants as small independent landholders.

In general nothing is said in discussions of land distribution about those who actually exploited the land – as if it could be assumed that those who owned the land and those who cultivated it were one and the same! This fact is the more striking in that the arrangements under which land was cultivated in France assuredly helped to establish for the French peasant a certain degree of independence with the result that a study of the system of cultivation seems to have the effect of reenforcing conclusions already drawn from a study of the distribution of land ownership. In central and eastern Europe the lords of the great estates had either kept or built up a very extensive domain which they exploited by means of forced labor imposed on their serfs. In England the great landholders by the process of dividing up and parceling out the common lands which was called "enclosure" had created extensive holdings which they exploited by means of agricultural day laborers. In France, the great landholder very rarely undertook the exploitation of his lands directly nor did he have recourse to the practice of enclosure and as a result he rented out his lands either for a monetary rent or on a share-cropping basis in various sized parcels but usually small, and usually as isolated segments of either tillable land, meadow land, or vineyard. Along with the peasant landholder accordingly there were to be found farm tenants and share-croppers and along with them peasants who supplemented their own holdings with lands (of different kinds or for different purposes) which they rented. Finally there were also agricultural day laborers who lived principally on their wages but who generally found some little corner or other of land to rent. In total there existed a very much greater variety of social conditions and differences in degree of independence than one would think from merely taking into consideration the actual ownership of property.

But these rather optimistic conclusions must be rather drastically qualified when two sets of facts which are ordinarily neglected are taken into account. From the point of view of its social and economic implications, the mere size of a piece of land either owned or farmed signifies nothing by itself. It assumes significance only if one compares it to the size of the average amount required to support a family of average size and thereby assure it of economic independence. The second fact that must be considered is that the total number of owners or tillers of land has significance only if compared to the total number of heads of families – a comparison which unfortunately involves a very large margin of error because of the lack of a methodical census. But however imperfect may be the results of these there is no room for doubt as to their general import. The proportion of those who tilled the land, and to an even greater degree the number of peasant landowners, who could live independently, without working for others, was very small in all parts of the country. Accordingly there was a very much larger group of peasants who owned or rented land but who did not have enough to live on and therefore were obliged either to carry on a trade or business or to hire out from time to time as day laborers in order to supplement their income. And finally there was a more or less considerable number of rural inhabitants who had only their wages to live on and when there was no work or the price of bread was too high, there was nothing left for them to do but to resort to begging. It is on this point that my opinion diverges most clearly from that of Loutchisky; he contrasted France, as a land of small proprietors, to England, as a land of free agricultural day laborers, and to easttern Europe, as a land of serfs where forced uncompensated labor was the rule. While this is correct as a rough generalization in comparing the different parts of Europe to one another, this contrast when made in this extreme fashion would seem to lead to the conclusion that the French peasant had enough land to support himself and that in this sense there was in our country no "agrarian problem." It was in fact quite otherwise: in certain regions such as maritime Flanders or in the vicinity of Versailles, heads of families lacking any property or rented land whatsoever amounted to an enormous majority (70 to 75%). In lower Normandy they amounted to at least a third if not more, and on the other hand, in areas where the pattern of land tenure was different, as on the plain of Picardy, the majority of owners and cultivators had only an amount that was clearly insufficient. At the end of the Old Regime, furthermore, the population was increasing very fast and accordingly the agrarian crisis was growing more acute.

This is manifest by the ardor with which the peasants encroached on the common lands or forests in order to build themselves a cottage or to clear small areas so as to add to their tillable land. The *cahiers* very often demanded the sale or lease of portions of the royal domain or even at least a part of the church lands. In this respect the agricultural proletariat and the peasants who already held land, but only an insufficient amount, were in agreement at least in principle. But the crisis also inspired complaints against the whole system of farm land tenure which seemed to come mostly from renters and share-croppers. They called for the dividing up of the great leaseholds and large blocks of land rented to agricultural entrepreneurs for profit, or at least they demanded that the number of small plots available not be decreased. Also they protested against the aggravation of the terms imposed on the leasers of land made possible by the heightening of competition induced by the greater pressure of need. In Picardy the "ill-will" which dated back to the sixteenth century or earlier intensified into a fury against anyone who had the misfortune to replace an evicted tenant. The petitions which were presented during the Revolution; the practices of certain rural communities the boundaries of which included a large proportion of nationalized church lands for which they succeeded in setting up a successful system of collective purchase so that they could be parceled out to small holders; certain practices with respect to communal lands like the *"portions menageres"* in Flanders and Artois which were let out only on life tenure for a rent paid to the community; or the temporary allotting of certain communal lands in Lorraine; all of these practices leave no doubt as to what was the more or less conscious ideal of the peasant masses. Each one was to have his share; a limited inequality does not seem to have been repugnant to them, especially since some of them were already above a condition of dire need, but there was a certain amount of land which was sufficient to support a family and no one ought to have more than that. Accordingly unused lands, those making up part of the royal domaine, those of the clergy (and later on those of the emigrés) were to serve to provide for the most unfortunate of the community.

. . . Still it should be emphasized that the "indigent" and the poor farmers did not think of property in exactly the same way as we do. As they did not have the means to buy the nationalized lands [when they were put up for sale during the Revolution], they demanded that they be leased out at the lowest rent possible, which would have secured for them the free disposition of their share at a small payment fixed once and for all while at the same time the nation would have still held them as ultimate owner, just as we have said the dividing up of common lands often saw the ultimate ownership of them reserved to the community. What mattered to the peasants was that they should enjoy the use of the land, the essential instrument of production.

But one would have a very incomplete idea of the limitations which the "common rights" of the peasants imposed on the rights of property if one stopped only with these observations. It is necessary at this point to recall that the "indigent" and the poor farmer only succeeded in subsisting thanks to the collective rights which, of course, the peasant in easy circumstances or even rich, benefited from as well as they, and even, ordinarily, very much more. There were, for example, the right of grazing cattle on lands where the grain had already been harvested and unenclosed fields; certain rights of usage of the forests; the enjoyment of the common rights of the community, such as the right of gleaning in harvested fields, and the right to collect stubble. Certain of these rights on the other hand could not be conceived of without a corresponding regulation of the actual cultivation of the land; the right of grazing cattle on harvested fields inevitably required that all the fields in a particular section be sown and harvested at the same time with the same crop; it automatically prevented the enclosing of fields. Because the rights of gleaning and gathering of stubble were very much less profitable if the scythe were used instead of the sickle, the owner was limited in the methods he used. And finally since the small farmer tilled the soil in order to gain a bare livelihood and like the people of the towns was always tortured by the fear of a shortage of food, which in view of the periodic shortages is very easy to understand, he frowned on the introduction of new crops in place of the familiar grains. He was no less ready than the townsman to prohibit not only the export and the hoarding of grain or any other device to stimulate a price rise, but also the free circulation of grain within France because there could never be too much grain in reserve in the barns. All the thinking of the poor peasant thus tended to limit the rights of individual property in order to defend collective usages which permitted him to live and which he regarded as a property right as sacred as that of others and one which existed to prevent the provisions necessary for his existence from becoming inaccessible to him. It little mattered to him that new arrangements would have increased production since it was he who would have had to pay the price of that progress, while all the benefits – or at least at the beginning – would have accrued to the large-scale farmers who either rented or owned their land and who produced for the market. In short, he opposed with all the force at his disposal the transformation of agriculture into a more capitalistic enterprise.

. . . Toward the middle of the eighteenth century, however, the example of England and the propaganda of the Physiocrats had given rise to a current of opinion in favor of reorganizing agriculture along more capitalistic lines. In order to do this it was necessary to do away with all regulation of cultivation and to grant the right to sell all products freely. It was necessary to suppress collective rights, especially the right of allowing cattle to graze in harvested fields which prevented their enclosure and to divide up the common lands among the inhabitants of the village to assure that this land would be cleared and utilized. The ministers of the king and the intendants made investigations, consulted together, and hesitated. The increase in production which the new theories promised them attracted them to the ideas: there would be no more food shortages, cattle would no longer need to be imported, and taxable commodities and population would increase along with food supply. But these administrators well realized that before attaining this golden age of capitalistic economy it would be necessary to go through a period of crisis which might last quite a long time. What would become of the peasants when they were deprived of a part of their resources? If the number of indigent increased, who would pay the taxes in their place? Were not troubles to be foreseen? The local officials, the municipal authorities and certain intendants, all of whom were in direct contact with the people and who were threatened with being blamed if riots broke out, all expressed reservations or showed themselves hostile to the new ideas. As controller-generals were changed, policy on this question often changed accordingly. This is well known in respect to free trade in grain: Bertin, Turgot and Brienne were in favor of it, Terray and Necker on two occasions favored regulation. M. Bloch has described the shifts in policy which prevented the enclosure and dividing up of the common lands from becoming general.

In general the royal administration visibly inclined, however, in favor of the innovators. There does not seem to be any doubt but that it was the interests of the privileged classes which swung the balance and it was that which aroused suspicion in the minds of the people against the transformation which was just getting underway. Most of the members of the privileged classes cared little for Physiocratic theory or increasing national production; they simply sought the best means to augment their incomes and, as the rise in prices and the rising requirements for luxurious living stimulated them, they had long ago taken the lead in this direction. Since the time of Louis XIV, under the cover of the ordinance of waters and forests, they had endeavoured to close their forests to the peasants, and the encroachment of the seigneurs on the common lands dated back at least to the sixteenth century. In any case, it does not appear to be contestable that during the last decades of the Old Regime, these tendencies were accentuated. The need doubtless became more and more pressing, but one cannot help but note that this economic offensive developed simultaneously with the aristocratic reaction against royal authority; the parlements which were so implacable toward the latter, never failed to place their authority at the service of the seigneurs. The theories of the Physiocratic economists very opportunely furnished the feudal interests with the pretext of serving the public good. As the price of wood rose more and more these interests, for example, carried on a bitter struggle against the common rights of the peasants to the use of the forests, and edicts closing the forests or limiting the common rights were handed down on the instigation of the great landed proprietors and accordingly it was they who profited from the situation. The consolidating of leasehold lands and the increase in the number of agricultural entrepreneurs who rented large tracts of land where sharecropping had previously prevailed was principally the work of these great proprietors. If the Physiocrats tended to make sacrosanct beings out of the great landed proprietors it was not just pure theory: these great proprietors were the members of the privileged classes.

But perhaps the most curious and least noted feature of this situation was that the tightening up of the feudal regime which was an indisputable characteristic of the eighteenth century, and especially the second half, stemmed from the same source.

To free himself from the bother of managing his estates and to assure himself of an increasing or at least a constant income, the seigneur leased out the right to collect the income from his feudal rights just as he farmed out in a block the right to his half of the crop of his share-croppers, or consolidated his leases in the hands of a large-scale leaseholder. This situation was not new, very far from it, but it became more and more frequent. But the one who under this arrangement was to actually collect the payments owed by the peasants naturally was rigorous in exacting them and attempted to increase them. In addition he speculated on the sale of the commodities which came to him as payments in kind. Nothing was more characteristic in this respect than what happened in the case of the forests and the seigneurs' right to graze cattle on the village lands which was peculiar to the eastern region of France and especially to Lorraine. The seigneur would lease out his right to cut wood and his tenant applied himself with zeal to the task of keeping out the peasants; he also leased his right to graze cattle, but whereas when he exercised it himself the peasant suffered very little since the seigneur only occasionally took advantage of it, when he leased out the right to a wealthy leaseholder who was sometimes even an important cattle dealer, everything changed and the village lands were invaded by an enormous herd. As a result the intrusion of capitalism into agriculture was made in part under the cover of feudal rights and made them very much more unbearable. It also perverted their very nature because they had been created to support a seigneur who lived in the midst of his peasants and now they passed into the hands of capitalists who thought only of deriving a profit from them.

But they also increased the income of the seigneur and thereby increased the value of his feudal rights in his eyes and his repugnance to abandon them. Even redemption itself would not have been agreeable to him for where could he invest the capital which he would have received from it? And what form of reinvestment would have offered the same security? The rise in prices combined with the new manner of capitalist exploitation of his feudal rights promised an indefinite increase while money loaned was subject to the risk of loss. But there was a basic conflict between the general intrusion of capitalism into agriculture and the maintenance of feudal rights and the payments made for the use of the land. The suppression of the common right to graze cattle in harvested fields, the fencing in of lands, and the freedom to plant various crops at will could only be obtained quickly if all lands were reassigned in such a way that the domain of the great proprietor, instead of being made up of scattered fields, was consolidated into a compact holding. This is what had been done in England beginning in the fifteenth and sixteenth centuries and especially in the eighteenth century and also in Germany in the first half of the nineteenth century. But in England that operation had been preceded by the disappearance of feudal rights in their literal form and the commutation of labor and monetary obligations into a rent of a fixed amount which had become of less and less importance as the puchasing power of money declined. It was of greater interest to the lord to consolidate his lands into large holdings than to conserve the old forms of tenure which prevailed. In central and eastern Europe for the most part these old forms of tenure had disappeared or had dwindled to insignificant proportions in the seventeenth and eighteenth centuries; the various feudal type payments were very much less productive than the lords' own domain lands. It is true that the labor obligations remained. But the lords contrived to oblige the peasants to redeem their payments and labor obligations by ceding to the lord a portion of their land. No longer having enough land to sustain them, they were then obliged to become day laborers. There was no longer any obstacle to redivision of the land. In France, on the contrary, the feudal rights and monetary obligations remained in existence; certain ground rents were still collected in kind and the conditions which had permitted enclosure in England did not therefore prevail. On the other hand, the domain lands of the seigneur had in very many villages been reduced almost to nothing with the result that the income from feudal rights constituted his principal revenue. In that case, one might say, what did it matter to him if a redivision of lands was made? It threatened him in that it would have completely overturned the forms of tenure on which the feudal edifice rested. In the process of exchanging his parcels of land for another portion in the village the peasant would have been able to contest certain rights and, as in England, the population would have been displaced as a result of this consolidation. And most importantly, very many of the seigneuries overlapped one another and how could one be sure of one's own in the confusion, or hope to carry out successfully such a complicated operation? Moreover, the peasant would have opposed it resolutely and the royal government which had its own interests and which was not as in England and in the monarchies of Eastern Europe subordinate to the aristocracy in law and fact, would never have consented to be constrained by the interests of that class. But it never had to take a stand on the issue because, as we have said, the seigneurs were too attached to their feudal rights to contemplate a general enclosure law. They did not fail to recognize its advantages and certain of them did carry out some partial redistributions by purchase or escheat when they had the opportunity, but this practice was always exceptional in the eighteenth century. Thus the few edicts of enclosure did not extend to all the provinces and exerted only a limited influence. They sufficed to irritate the peasant but did not succeed in giving to agriculture the impulsion in the direction of capitalism which it had received in England. Our rural people wished to be rid of the feudal obligations, but they did not suspect that thanks to them they had escaped the terrible fate which the enclosure movement had brought to the English farmer and still held in store for the Prussian peasant. Perhaps they would not have been able to avoid it if the Old Regime had lasted longer. The king might have finally been able to arrange for the redemption of feudal rights as the king of Sardinia had done already, or perhaps the progress of capitalism would have convinced the aristocracy itself that it was to its advantage to bring it about in order to finance the newly rising industry and to make enclosure possible. The events of 1789 saved the French peasant and in spite of appearances his influence was just as conservative as it was revolutionary. He overturned the feudal regime but he consolidated the agrarian structure of France.

IV

The capitalistic transformation of agriculture should not in principle have had the effect of engendering antagonism between the aristocracy and the bourgeoisie, but indeed rather solidarity. One should only note that the former had a very much greater interest in it than the latter because the latter at the end of the Old Regime possessed only relatively few landed estates. The conflict arose when it came to the question of feudal rights and land rents. The clerical tithe was of little importance. The upper clergy defended it tenaciously for it constituted a very considerable portion of its revenues. But only a very small portion of the nobility was interested in maintaining the "subinfeudated" tithes and actually the lay aristocracy made no effort to come to the aid of the ecclesiastical aristocracy on this point.

But, as has been said, it thought otherwise about feudal rights while the bourgeoisie, in principal, were hostile to them. They presented an obstacle to the introduction of capitalist modes of production which required freedom for the individual and hence the suppression of serfdom; economic freedom and hence the abolition of the *banalités* and other seigneurial monopolies; the consolidation of the home market hence the abolition of tolls; the mobility of capital and hence the extinction of primogeniture, of escheat, of reversion of property to next of kin, of the right of *franc-fief*. Obligations paid in kind and the clerical tithe also stood in the way of the rationalization of farming methods: they especially deprived the lands of the straw which should have returned to them in the form of manure. Finally, as has been shown, the whole system of feudal rights required the maintenance of tenures as they existed and made impossible the redistribution of lands and hence the large-scale methods of cultivation which are natural to a capitalistic organization of agriculture.

A part at least of the great noblemen and certainly the liberal noblemen who played such an important role in the opening phases of the Revolution, doubtless would not have refused to propose in the *cahiers* the redemption of feudal rights and even the abolition without indemnity of the more oppressive ones. The resistance to this developed rather among the petty noblemen who lived primarily on their feudal payments and who remained attached to the military character and the traditional idleness of the French nobility. They were frightened at the idea that they, like the bourgeoisie, would have to find profitable investment for the money which they would receive from redemption, which would mean that they would no longer be "living nobly." Besides, once their monetary rights disappeared, how could they hope to retain their honorific prerogatives? The nobleman did not wish to become a citizen like any other; he did not wish to pay taxes like any bourgeois and he wished even less to find himself on a footing of equality with his peasants. It was under these circumstances that combined action by the peasantry and the bourgeoisie became possible on the day when the privileged classes in the Estates General refused to join with the deputies of the Third Estate, that is to say, with the bourgeoisie. But if the bourgeoisie while at odds with both the Court and the aristocracy could not afford to be disdainful of the support of the peasants, it certainly did not think of calling them to a revolt against their seigneurs, nor even to concede to them by legal means the abolition without indemnity of their feudal dues. Among the members of the Constituent Assembly there were many lawyers who looked on these rights as an individual property as legitimate as any other, and one which could not be destroyed without placing the bourgeoisie itself in peril. Many of these were feudal lawyers by profession, like Merlin de Douai, or judges, collectors, or business agents of seigneurs, and they were in no hurry to jeopardize the source of their incomes. In addition, the nobles were not the only ones who possessed seigneuries: more than one had passed into the hands of bourgeois owners.

But the peasant took his cause into his own hands, as we have said, and settled the issue by refusing to pay his feudal obligations as well as the clerical tithe, and by burning up the records and even in some cases the *châteaux*. Not being in a position to alienate him, the bourgeoisie along with the liberal members of the nobility, granted him on the night of August 4, the pure and simple abolition of part of the feudal obligations and the redemption of those which represented a rent for the use of land. To the degree that the conflict between the nobility and the triumphant bourgeoisie intensified, the former had to agree to more and more extensive concessions. After the uprising of August 10, 1792, the latter suppressed without indemnity the payments for which a specific legal title could not be produced and after that of June 2, 1793 it decreed the complete abolition of all obligations without any reservations.

. . . There was then an autonomous peasant revolution. It must be distinguished from the revolution of the bourgeoisie just as that is differentiated from the revolution of the aristocracy and the popular democratic revolution from that of the wealthy landowner.

With these facts in mind a few reflexions

of the greatest importance cannot fail to occupy our minds. The economic interpretation of history (inappropriately designated by the name "historical materialism" which I have never found in Marx) is given too narrow an interpretation when the French Revolution is made to evolve solely from the rise of the bourgeoisie. It arose also out of the resistance which the privileged classes opposed to the rise of a new economic order, or, to put it better, out of their resolve to reap the benefits of it themselves. But it had its origin equally in the opposition of the least favored classes to the capitalistic order which had begun to be established. If they were so bitter against the aristocracy it was not only because the feudal regime had always oppressed them, but also because the capitalistic spirit had little by little penetrated the aristocracy itself and thus had rendered the feudal regime the more hateful. But it does not follow from this that they were to the least degree sympathetic toward capitalism or that they fought in order to establish it. But it happened that the emergence of this new social order provoked hostile reactions, which nevertheless at the same time favored its ultimate triumph. To the extent that the Old Regime was forced to adopt policies favorable to capitalism in order to satisfy the economic aspirations of the bourgeoisie, it contributed very effectively to the preparation of its own ruin.

THE SOURCES OF SOCIAL CONFLICT IN 1789

FRÉDÉRIC BRAESCH

Having devoted a long and productive scholarly career since the turn of the century to the history of the Revolution, Frédéric Braesch has long been respected by other scholars in the field. His work on the financial history of the Revolution has been especially valuable. Although the book from which the following excerpt is taken deals only with the year 1789 it, in effect, is an attempt at an interpretive study of the whole Revolutionary movement since M. Braesch thinks that the main lines of development for the whole period were largely determined by the events of that year.

ALONG with the incitements of the political theorists, the possibility of class conflict constituted another danger. And the latter was perhaps the graver threat of the two since feudal despotism was doubtless more hated by the vast bulk of the population than ministerial despotism. As pointed out in the preceding chapter, neither the abolition of serfdom, nor of feudal proprietory rights, nor the legal suppression of honorific privileges appeared at first to give rise to any unalterable opposition on the part of the privileged classes which had, for their own part, voluntarily declared themselves ready to renounce their tax privileges. Two serious threats none the less seemed likely to endanger the peaceful relations of the classes in the very near future.

The first danger was that the masses might be carried along by the contagion of example toward the denial of all social rank and distinction which in turn might lead to the arbitrary suppression of even the most legitimate of rights if their existence was in any way likely to stand in the way of the leveling instincts of the populace. . . .

There were, however, still other reasons for the privileged classes to fear their former tenants and these more serious than just the threat of the passing away of class distinctions. In addition to matters of decorum, social conflict had its economic aspect. The rising cost of living for one thing and property rights for another. Especially the question of property rights. As always happens, the overturn of the social hierarchy carried with it the risk of bringing to the fore the question of property itself, and under the cover of demands calling for the more or less complete abolition of the last feudal rights, there was reason to fear the pressing of claims of an entirely different kind.

There was not yet, however, in this instance the same danger from radical theories, as there was in the case of the political threat. The very principle of individual property rights was not threatened as was the principle of absolutism by the theorists and the "makers of systems." The first pamphleteers of the Revolution were not partisans of the "agrarian law" about which there was to be so much controversy a few years later. . . . Before Babeuf, the ideas which we call "socialistic" did not appear in the history of the French Revolu-

From Frédéric Braesch, *1789, L'année cruciale* (Paris, 1941), Chapter II, pp. 59–74. Translated by the Editor. By permission Librairie Gallimard.

tion. This is seemingly the result of the little interest of Frenchmen in general in problems of social economics. The fact that Babeuf, our first socialist theoretician, had followed the profession of *"commissaire à terrier"* and thus found himself naturally concerned with these questions by his professional obligations, is significant in this regard.

There was then at the beginning of the Revolution, little reason to fear that a few socialist theoreticians would excite the people to the destruction of the capitalist regime on which nearly all societies have been founded from antiquity up to the present day. But in such matters there is no need of learned theories and subtle reasoning to excite the covetousness of the disinherited. "Hedonistic savagery" constitutes in itself a grave danger in all societies where the different classes are in a state of unstable equilibrium. Was this the case in 1789, and, if so, in what form did the question of class conflict present itself?

In the first place, as has been true in nearly all times, it revolved around the question of the division of property and the ownership of the land (France being then almost entirely an agricultural country). This then is the question which has to be studied first even though it can be said at once that the answer to it will not in itself suffice to explain the importance of social strife on the eve of the Revolution. This can be explained only by going beyond this to the question of the financial obligations owed by the peasant landholder which had recently become more burdensome and consequently gave a greater urgency to peasant protests against them.

With respect to the division of property, there does not appear to have been much difference between the situation on the eve of the Revolution and that at the end of the reign of Louis XIV. It is possible that the share of the two privileged orders had slightly decreased in the course of the century, but we have no precise information on the matter. We cannot in all cases enumerate with certainty the proportion of landowners to renters on the eve of the Revolution. This question has been very much discussed and numerous works have produced some interesting details. But in the absence of a uniform and complete enumeration it is impossible to give a definite answer. The answer, moreover, depends first on the definition that should be given to the word "owner" during the Old Regime. In the feudal hierarchy, the seigneur, which is to say the titular possessor of a seigneurie or *"circonscription elementaire"* held as a fief, was considered in the Middle Ages to be the true owner of all the lands of the seigneurie. Aside from the lands which were farmed by him by means of the *corvée* and which constituted his domain, all the rest was divided into holdings farmed by the holder as kind of a tenant or lessor with the leases in effect being guaranteed in perpetuity through the medium of an annual payment or ground-rent (*cens*) the amount of which was fixed once and for all. From this viewpoint, all the lands in the kingdom would have had as owners either a member of the nobility, a churchman, or a chapter of a religious community. The old allodial lands having nearly disappeared it would have almost been literally true that there was no land without a seigneur. But as is well known, with the establishment of the communes which were considered to be a kind of collective seigneurie, it became possible for there to be seigneur owners who were neither noblemen nor ecclesiastics. The two first orders could not then be considered, even from the theoretical viewpoint which has just been described and which was that of the feudal lawyers, as owners of the *whole* of the lands of the kingdom. It is clear, however, that for those who reasoned in this way, the vast majority of the lands of the kingdom had to belong to members of the nobility or the clergy. It was on the basis of this reasoning that the Third Committee of the Second Assembly of Notables convoked by Louis XVI made the following declaration in an opinion given in response to the fifth question submitted to it for its examination:[1] "One is easily convinced that in the matter of land ownership, the first two orders hold perhaps more than two thirds" (opinion given December 10, 1788). Going on they said, "Almost all rural properties are only the concession of various seigneurs who, having reserved with respect to these concessions the right to some form of payment or quit-rent, are still the eminent proprietors of them."

Since the twelfth or thirteenth century, however, many changes had taken place, not only in the persons of the seigneurs or the farming tenants, but also in the situation of the latter. In the course of time many tenants paying ground-rent had freed themselves from the payment of this, either in a legal fashion by purchase, or simply in fact. These "free tenants" were thus fully owners. On the other hand certain tenants holding by payment of ground-rent (that is to say holding their lands directly from the seigneur) had more land than they could till and so rented it out in turn. And so, although liable for payment of the seigneurial *cens,* they appear to be in some respects, at least, like owners of the part which they rent out in turn. But it should be especially noted that a holder by *cens* was not like an ordinary renter; he could not be dispossessed of his lands, he could pass them on to his heirs, he could will them, or give them away, or sell them, and, as we have just indicated, he could rent them out at will. From the point of view of economic and social realities as opposed to the purely juridical point of view of the feudal lawyers, all holders by *cens* ought to be considered as owners. This principle, established by Loutchisky, but contested by Kovalevsky, seems to be universally accepted today. Its application of course decreases very greatly the proportion of the land owned by the first two classes.

That, however, raises another question: among the actual farming peasants what was the proportion of owners defined in the manner we have just indicated, to ordinary renters? Or, in other words, did there exist before the Revolution a significant group of *small peasant landowners?*

When one repeats the well-known fact that the Revolution was the occasion of a transfer of property on a grand scale, it is too often imagined that it caused property to pass from the hands of the nobility and the clergy into those of the peasants and that out of their holdings there was created the small peasant landowner. But the study in recent years of the sale of the nationalized lands has made it evident that the despoiling of the noble or ecclesiastical proprietor as a result of that sale redounded to the profit, not of the actual tiller of the land, but simply of another proprietor who rented the land out – but this time a member of the Third Estate. It is necessary, however, to go even further and to abandon that idea which has been blindly accepted for too long, to the effect that the landowners of the Old Regime were for the most part either from the privileged classes or town-dwelling bourgeoisie and consequently few in number.

Here no more than in most other instances has a new idea been immediately accepted when first presented. It is because the traditional view which it contradicts is based on the evidence of a great many of the *cahiers* and for a long time historians have been used to considering the *cahiers* of 1789 as a source of unimpeachable value. When at the very end of the last century suggestions were made that on questions of land tenure the *cahiers* should be checked against the registers of the *vingtième,* the learned author of the publication dealing with the convocation of the Estates General of 1789, Armand Brette along with Edmé Champion took upon themselves the task of demonstrating the complete uselessness if not outright inaccuracy of this new form of evidence. However, in spite of some more or less conscious errors (made to favor the well-to-do owners) which the lists of the payers of the *vingtième* might contain (errors which affect moreover only the esti-

[1] The fifth question was as follows: "What ought to be the respective number of deputies for each order? Should the number be equal for each order?

mates of the *value* of the various properties), they are still useful for determining the amount of land held since these measurements were made by different officials than those who made the valuations (these are actual measurements rather than estimates as in the case of valuations and furnish precise and reliable figures). These are obviously more reliable than the interested and more or less exaggerated complaints which the peasants made in 1789 when they were desirous of painting as dark a picture as possible of their condition in the hope of obtaining as many advantages as possible for the improvement of their lot.

As between the number of tenants noted in the lists of the *vingtième* and those claimed in the *cahiers,* there can be no hesitation as to which is the more reliable. The *cahiers* continue to be useful as an auxiliary source, but one should begin with the lists. But the works based on the latter, and notably the studies of Loutchisky, have demonstrated that the small peasant owner was not in the least a creation of the Revolution but existed before that event. It must be recognized that these studies have, in fact, brought out a number of very suggestive figures. They have, for example, established the fact that only 17% of the peasants in two *districts* of Limousin were not landowners.

The method followed by Loutchisky has, however, rightly been criticized for counting as owners all individuals possessing any portion of land whatsoever, however small it might have been (for example, an orchard or a garden, etc.), even when the owner could not have lived off it. In addition, it is true that a few isolated instances like, for example, the two *elections* of Limousin which comprise only a small fraction of the whole country, cannot support conclusions about the whole kingdom. Many scholars have carried on the work of the Russian historians and studies like those of MM. Bloch, Marion, Seé, Laude, Donat, Schmitt, Porée, Martin, Nicolle, and G. Lefebvre have contributed to the extension and greater precision of our knowledge. Their research has been very much more useful than all the reasoning which one might try to do *a priori.* To say, for example, that the proportion of peasant proprietors *must have* increased in the course of the 18th century because a number of the latter have by reducing their standard of living been able to buy off the *cens,* is not very convincing. It could easily be shown that the trend was in the opposite direction because some seigneurs extended their domain land by purchases – and we cannot say which of the two trends was predominant. But from some of the works just cited we can derive some conclusions worthy of reliance even if not absolutely definitive.

"The first thing that is apparent," wrote M. G. Lefebvre in an excellent article based on a study which he undertook a dozen years ago relative to this question, "is that the agrarian map of France in 1789 is characterized by extreme variety. From one region to another the amount of land owned by the nobility varies between nine and forty-four percent; it is rare for that of the clergy to exceed twenty percent but it goes below that figure in more than one instance; the proportion owned by the bourgeoisie ranges from twelve to forty-five percent; that of the peasants from twenty-two to seventy percent." It can be seen as the result of averaging the extreme figures that the portion held by the clergy was the smallest of all – contrary to what one would have expected. M. Lefebvre estimates that "for the whole of France it never exceeded one tenth." Thus the sale of ecclesiastical property could not possibly have constituted the inexhaustible source of wealth which the Constituent Assembly represented it to be. The shares of the nobility and the bourgeoisie were very nearly equal and even when added together make for less than half the total. As for the share of the peasantry, it was at least equal to the preceding two put together, but varied enormously depending on the region. It was greater in the areas which were originally forested and in the mountains, which is to say, where the clearing had been done by individuals. It was very low on the contrary in the areas where large-scale effort had been necessary prior to cultivation—like the draining of swamps which could only be undertaken by abbeys or persons having at their disposal substantial capital. It was low also in the environs of the large cities where the owners were either noble or bourgeois. Taken all together, the proportion owned by the peasants must have been in the neighborhood of *half* of the arable land.

On the other hand it is most important to emphasize that the holdings of the peasants were generally very small in size and accordingly there was a very large number of tiny individual farming units. Peasant property was so very cut up that most of that class owned only very small lots. In most instances their holding was too small to support them and consequently they had to hire themselves out as farm laborers or carry on a trade on the side (according to Loutchisky only 18% of the peasant proprietors could afford to live without recourse to outside employment). On the other hand among the privileged classes and the bourgeoisie even though the lands naturally were divided among a very much smaller number of owners, each estate was made up of a collection of parcels of land of small- or medium-sized extent; large compact holdings were rare. Most of the large-scale consolidated capitalistic farming enterprises (whether run by owners or renters) were then of little importance. Thus as between the type of agricultural organization of eastern Europe (great estates exploited directly by the lord by means of serfs subjected to forced labor) and that of England (large estates worked by free men but reduced to the condition of landless day laborers working for the owner of the estate) France, to which should be added the Rhineland area of Germany, constituted a third unique type. It was a farm economy characterized on the one hand by a relatively large number of peasant owners, and on the other hand by the fragmentation into a great many isolated lots even of the lands which remained in the hands of the privileged classes and the bourgeoisie, that is to say, of non-exploiting owners.

That situation which already foreshadowed that which prevails today (it is well known that France is a land of innumerable small landowners and of multiple little farming units) does not seem at first glance to have been one that should have aroused any very sharp social conflict such as one might have expected, on the contrary, in the case of a land of large estates and a large agricultural proletariat whether of servile or free condition. But it was precisely in France, and in France alone, that a formidable explosion was to take place. Nothing, however, seemed to foreshadow it at the beginning of the year 1789. No one among the peasantry thought of protesting against the very principle of property which they were all very respectful of: the simple day laborers would not have dared raise their voices when the *cahiers* were being drawn up, and it was the voice of the small peasant proprietor which alone made itself heard. This group admitted very willingly that one should pay rent for land since a number of them let out all or part of their own holdings on lease. As for the tenant farmers, they found it natural to pay their rent to the owner of their land whether he was a peasant, bourgeois, noble or ecclesiastic. Thus, it was not with respect to the principle of property itself that the question of social conflict was raised with such particular sharpness in 1789. And yet it was raised. Under what circumstances?

One might be tempted to attribute to actual misery or want, the profound discontent of the peasant masses. It is certain that there was throughout the country a great deal of misery: "In the north, the inquest of 1790 estimated at one fifth the number of indigent *in normal times.*" The cause for this lay, in part at least, in the extremely small scale of the farming units which limited the farmer to traditional methods and prevented technical progress; in part to the fact that a great number of peasants had not sufficient land to support themselves, and in part also to the incontestable increase in the population and the inability of the government at that time to give work to an appreciable number of men. The want which was indeed severe, moreover, was greater in 1788–9 than in previous years, and what was worse, the cost of living had not ceased to rise during the several preceding decades as will be shown presently. It was this want which at this time impelled a large number of unfortunates to become beggars, smugglers, thieves or to form real bands of "wanderers." But if there was some misery, and even real want, how many times had our country not experienced many situations more terrible yet! These particular but passing circumstances without doubt aggravated the crisis, but they did not create it.

In seeking the causes of conflict, one might also think of the lure of the great estates to the peasant who had too little land to live on and was always trying to extend his holdings. But we have said that the great estate was the exception, and yet the crisis broke out across the whole country. The true cause of the latter must be sought elsewhere.

What produced this crisis and made it so serious was precisely the fact which at first sight would seem to make it inexplicable: it was precisely the existence of a very large number of small landowners who were *attached to the very principle of property*. It was not, indeed, in order to get possession of the property of others that they protested, but to free themselves from the obligations which they did not believe they owed. That was the aim of these free landowners and their opposition was reminiscent of that of the small artisan of the faubourg Saint Antoine in Paris rather than that of the proletarian masses in certain other of the poorer quarters of the capital.

When we started out above to examine the question of peasant property on the eve of the Revolution, we said that the first difficulty to be overcome in this study lay in the very problem of defining property at this time. For the feudal lawyer, the true owner was the seigneur who collected the quit-rents, and the tenants who held on the terms of payment of a ground rent were simply renters; to them the *cens* was nothing more nor less than a rent for the land. For the peasant, however, a tenant paying ground rent who had effective rights of disposition of his land as master, was, in fact, the true owner of it and the *cens* therefore was not a true rent payment but one of those feudal obligations, one of those outdated symbols of lordship which were held in horror by the men of the countryside and the abolition of which they demanded.

Whether the *cens* represented a true rent or a feudal obligation, his practical interest in the question was, in the first place, whether the tenant would be obligated to the seigneur for its redemption even after the suppression of the so-called feudal rights, or whether he would be freed of it entirely by this suppression. In general the peasants had for a long time pressed for the diminution or suppression, as with the other vestiges of the hated feudal regime, of the greatest possible part of the payments which they paid to the privileged, while the latter, on the contrary, tried to figure out ways to increase the payments in order to increase their revenues. The latter was a relatively recent development in the attitude of the two first orders toward the peasant, and it is in that change that one must look for the factor which made social conflict particularly menacing in 1789. It was from that source that was to come the danger of "hedonistic savagery" in the event that all barriers were broken down and all authority weakened. Most of the actual farming peasants, whether they ought truly to be considered owners, renters, or sharecroppers, could indeed constitute a grave danger to social peace and order, if the obligations demanded from them by the first two orders on any basis whatsoever became more burdensome or were more impatiently borne.

That seems, however, to have indeed been the case on the eve of the Revolution and it is with respect to this question of the relatively greater weight of these obligations that the situation at this time reveals itself as manifestly more serious than at any other moment in the course of the century. Doubtlessly the *cahiers* protested only against feudal rights and not against property rights, but it was difficult in practice to make this distinction and those whose interests were involved certainly hoped to see the various dues which they had to pay perceptibly decreased, whatever their origin and character — and sometimes they were mixed together indiscriminately and confused in the very registers where they were recorded.

This attitude could only have proceeded from a relatively recent aggravation of the burden of these obligations. But this last point has been disputed. In a study entitled *La féodalité sous Louis XVI,* A. Aulard maintained that "there is no certainty . . . as to whether in fact this feudal burden was aggravated." First he cites the edict of 1779 providing for the abolition of serfdom and the right of mainmorte in the crown lands, as well as the seigneurs' right of pursuit of his own serfs. Then he recalls that the *cens,* the seigneurial right *par excellence,* the preeminent symbol of lordship, had remained at the same level as in the 17th and 16th centuries which in effect meant a lightening of the burden because of the persistent inflation. And finally he cites a few cases of seigneurs who exercised their rights with moderation. But in support of the opposing viewpoint, M. Sagnac . . . has shown that the king and the seigneurs sought in the 18th century to extend their rights by resuming old ones which had lapsed or by trying to impose new ones which they claimed they had always been entitled to. That which does appear to be proved conclusively is that, whatever may have been the reason, many of the registers (*terriers*) in which these obligations were recorded were revised or renewed under Louis XVI, and especially during the decade immediately preceding the beginning of the Revolutionary movement.

Such a revision of the registers was, however, nothing new: it is recognized that since the 17th century the seigneurs had demanded from their vassals "declarations" and "accountings" at more or less regular intervals — a proceeding made necessary by the changes which had taken place in the meantime in the names of the tenants holding by *cens* as a result of new divisions, or sales, or for any other reason. A renewal of the *terriers* between 1780 and 1789 was not then in itself anything unusual. But, as A. Aulard recognized, it did have the effect of increasing, at least nominally, the revenues of the seigneurs. And even if this effect was not as general as some scholars have tried to maintain, it is none the less certain that several instances have been found of the seigneurs encouraging their agents who were revising the *terriers* to make some "discoveries" of new or lapsed payments that were owed by promising them a percentage of the increase in the event of success.

The proof that this renewal of the land registers was almost universal and that it must necessarily have been the principle cause of discontent on the eve of the Revolution, lies in the fact that every area where it definitely had not taken place, which is to say in certain regions in the western part of the kingdom, the peasants did not have toward their seigneurs the same attitude of hostility and hatred as was found in all the rest of the kingdom. This was most notably true in the region of the Vendée, where the *terriers* had been renewed since time immemorial at the same rates, and as a result of progressive inflation these had ended up being very light. As a result the peasants paid them very willingly, looking at them as a kind of rent which merely gave recognition to the seigneur of his right of property. The feeling among them that this was a debt legitimately contracted with the latter was so strong that a few years later when the Revolution was in full swing, and when the land of the *emigrés* was being sold by the government, these peasant tenants are found, after first paying their rent on their farm to the new owner, then turning around and paying it a second time as a matter of conscience to the former seigneur, whose imprescriptible rights and legitimate ownership they thereby recognized. This fact demonstrates better than anything else could how low these dues were for the time, for it is only reasonable that those who paid them thus benevolently a second time would not have been able to do so if the payment in question had been of a significant amount. But this popularity of the nobility of the region of the Vendée was an exception resulting from the particularly humane manner in which the seigneurs of this area had treated their tenants. Elsewhere, moreover, the disaffection of the people of the countryside toward their social superiors is the irrefutable proof of a treatment quite the opposite, and in the rest of the kingdom, the embittered peasants, very far from considering these payments as amounts legitimately owed for the rent of the land, saw in them only symbols of the abhorred feudalism, and pridefully looked upon themselves as the true owners of the lands which they cultivated.

It was then, in our opinion, this revision of the land registers, which had moreover been going on intensively for only about the preceding ten years, along with the fact that it coincided with the increasingly heavy obligations of payers of the *cens* toward the royal government (they had been very appreciably increased, for example, by royal order as late as August 20, 1786) — it was this combination of factors — which had intensified the peasant's hate of feudalism and his feudal lords on the eve of the Revolution.

Some other reasons may also have contributed to an aggravation of their discontent such as the general rise in prices, which marked the second half of the 18th century and which, according to the extended researches of M. Labrousse, affected our country particularly in the period 1785–1789. This rise was probably caused by an increase in the amount of money in circulation. Without doubt since the time of the financial catastrophe caused by John Law at the beginning of the century, this had not been due to an increase of paper money as such. But credit needs had required the use of drafts, bills of exchange, letters of credit, etc., which took the place of an actual paper currency. Under Louis XVI, moreover, the *Caisse D'Escompte* had resumed the issue of real bank notes, and as a result of the edict of August 18, 1788 which suspended the payment of certain government interest obligations in hard cash, the government had even returned to the system of Law to the extent of issuing paper notes payable to the bearer, although not transferable. Thus at the time of the meeting of the Estates General these *billet de caisse* in a limited sense (they were legal tender only in Paris) already foreshadowed the *assignats*. In the spring of 1789, however, the money that was used everywhere and every day was overwhelmingly metallic currency, the value of the individual pieces of which had not been altered since the edicts of 1726 (a value already — if not quite — that established by the Revolutionary government in the month of Germinal, 1797). Accordingly one can no longer think of attributing to manipulation of the currency, the most frequent and most important cause for fluctuations in prices, the general rise in the cost of living on the eve of the Revolution.

But there had been in France in the 18th century, and especially in the last half of the century, a real superabundance of metallic currency. There had indeed been struck in our country, 2 billion, 446 and a half million pieces of gold and silver between 1726 and 1780, because France alone had retained at that time half of the precious metals entering Europe during that period, and the mineral production of the world during the 18th century was, for gold, more than the total production during the two preceding centuries, and for silver almost eight tenths of the latter. But this increase in the means of payment was very much more rapid than that of the stocks of merchandise available. The development of industry in France, stopped on the eve of the Seven Years War, was resumed in a small way under Louis XVI, but we were very much behind England in this respect, from whom we had just barely begun to borrow the machine. On the other hand, the introduction of these machines required for the creation of these capital goods (that is to say non-consumable goods and goods not yet in themselves productive of more consumable goods) a great quantity of consumption goods for which the demand was already tending to exceed the supply.

In any case, and in whatever way it may be explained, the end result, a general rise in prices, is an incontestable fact. According to M. Labrousse it attained during the period 1785–89, 65% of the index of the period 1726–41 taken by him for a base. This amounts to saying that instead of the 100 *livres* which it cost to buy various products about 1740, it was necessary to pay 165 *livres* in 1789. Moreover this increase applied especially to foodstuffs and above all to bread, which, according to M. Labrousse, made up at least half of the expenses of the average household.

This general rise in prices certainly was to some degree responsible for the great increase in the resentment of the masses. While the increase in the costs of the necessities of life amounted to 65%, the average wage, still following M. Labrousse, increased only 22%. The wage earner thus saw his purchasing power diminished about 26% or a good quarter, which amounts to saying that he had become perceptibly worse off. And this fact is indeed confirmed by the testimony of foreigners like Arthur Young, who is always so clear and categorical in what he says, and whose testimony can be accepted on this point, although in general he ought to be used with caution because he compares France of 1789, not with the France of 1740, but with the England of 1789. In addition, we know that the population of France had certainly increased noticeably in the 18th century and the surplus of labor available could only have had the effect of lowering the average level of wages.

Wage earners, however, did not constitute the whole working population of France, and in addition, in this country which was still three fourths agricultural, out of the 15 to 20 millions of peasants which one can count, the proletarians (agricultural day laborers or mendicants to which should be added the serfs), Lavoisier believed, amounted to only about five million. Although certain modern scholars would make the figure appreciably larger, it is still none the less certain that it was the non-proletarian (small farm owners or renters) who constituted the backbone of the peasant class. But the condition of this non-wage-earning element would certainly not have been made worse by the increase in the cost of living (very far from it since they took in 65% more on the sale of their products and paid only 22% more to their hired hands) if they had not on the other hand seen the charges which they had to pay to the seigneur very appreciably increased – and this brings us again to the question of the renewal of the land registers.

Not only, indeed, were all the workers not wage earners, but not even all Frenchmen were workers. But the increase in the cost of living affected everyone, and it fell more heavily on those who lived on the work of others (the privileged classes) than on the producers who possessed consumable goods on which the price could be increased at will. The latter, which is to say the peasants, were selling their products at higher prices and those who lived on payments made by them, following their example, tried to increase these in turn.

In the case of non-noble land and a non-noble owner the peasant renter could say nothing and did not even think of protesting, since he would be the first to recognize the legitimacy of property rights. But when the peasant had facing him as his landlord not a commoner but a nobleman, he could think of arguing about the nature of the payment demanded from him, refusing to see in it a true rent for a leasehold but rather looking on it as one of those feudal obligations which everyone was calling for an end to.

Whether the increase in rents paid by the peasants to noble or bourgeois landowners actually amounted to as much as 98% as M. Labrousse maintains, while prices for foodstuffs went up only 65%; or to put it another way, whether the landowning classes had actually benefited from an increase in income of this magnitude, is a point which remains doubtful.[2] But what is more important is that the question is put wrong. The agrarian crisis which actually erupted did not have, in fact, the character which a simple reading of these figures would seem to suggest that it had: it was not an attack of the servile classes provoked by the sight of the rich getting richer at the expense of the still impoverished poor. That certain rich men, very rich men, privileged or nonprivileged, were able to increase their wealth under these circumstances is indeed very possible. But beside them, there were how many little seigneurs who had never been rich who were threatened by the rise in the cost of living with the prospect of starvation, because their class prejudice prevented them from working? The sharpness with which they pressed the revision of the *terriers* was often on their part only the result of an imperious necessity.

As for the peasants, the question of whether or not, taking into account all the factors (a decline in the wages paid to those whom they occasionally employed; an increase in the value of the farm products sold by them; an increase in the obligations owed to a nobleman or a bourgeois owner), they gained or lost in comparison to their previous condition is of little importance in explaining their hostility. For, whoever knows the peasant character – avid for gain, and grudging in its expenditures – it is not difficult to conceive the effect which was produced by an increase in his annual payments, and especially where it was accomplished by that revision of the *terriers* which was undertaken by the privileged classes during the decade immediately preceding the Revolution.

This process of renewal caused lively discontent among the masses of peasants whose interests clashed directly with those making the revisions. Undoubtedly at the time of the drawing up of the *cahiers* care was taken to distinguish between the obligations owed to the seigneur as landowner and the sums owed as feudal charges. But more than one of these simple souls was dissatisfied with merely putting in writing these minimum claims, and nursed a smouldering resentment against the seigneur and his chateau on account of the accursed *terriers*. The closer they lived to the seigneur and the smaller personage he was, the more lively was their rancor, for in this situation he pressed his peasants out of bitter necessity and was more harsh in his exactions. They came to hate him personally because they dealt with him directly almost every day whereas the great seigneur living at court, the bishop, or the religious community they dealt with only through the intermediary of a business agent who drew to himself all their hatred.

It was inevitable that when authority relaxed and the forces of law and order weakened, an example having been given somewhere in the kingdom, France would explode as though a powder train had been lit and everywhere across the countryside following attacks by the peasants on the *châteaux*, one would see the sky reddened by the glow of fires burning up the *terriers*.

[2] If the wealth of the upper classes had increased, they would have increased their expenditures for luxuries. But it has been shown that the luxury trades experienced numerous failures in the years 1780–1785. It is to be presumed that deceived by the earlier increases – only nominal and not real – in the income of the well-to-do classes, certain traders had hoped to make more money by increasing their stocks. The subsequent failure of many of them is proof that their calculation was wrong and that the increase in the wealth of the affluent classes was more apparent than real.

SUGGESTIONS FOR ADDITIONAL READING

Although we are favored from time to time with excellent translations of important works dealing with the French Revolution, it still remains true that it is impossible to read deeply into any special aspect of this subject without a reading knowledge of French. The books bearing on this problem which are available in English will be listed first for convenience.

The student interested in reading further on this problem should begin by reading G. Lefebvre's *Quatre-vingt-neuf* (Paris, 1939) in its excellent English translation by R. R. Palmer, published under the title, *The Coming of the French Revolution* (Princeton, N. J., 1947), and now available in a paperbound edition (New York, 1957). This is by far the best introduction to the social and economic history of the Old Regime in France. The student should then go on to read all of Alexis de Tocqueville's *The Old Regime and the French Revolution,* originally published as *L'ancien régime et la Révolution française* (Paris, 1856), in any one of its several translations. The paperbound edition translated by Stuart Gilbert and published by Doubleday Anchor (Garden City, N. Y., 1955) is excellent in every respect. This classic is a mine of information and its glossary of many of the terms used in connection with the seigneurial regime is especially useful to the student. Another book, portions of which have been used in the foregoing text, that should be read in its entirety is Henri Sée's *Economic and Social Conditions in France During the Eighteenth Century,* translated by E. Zeydel (New York, 1927). This contains much information on industry, the guilds, and working classes, as well as on the peasants.

There are a few older general treatments of the subject in English which are now more or less outdated but which might be useful for some details. One of these is E. J. Lowell's *The Eve of the French Revolution* (Boston, 1892), and another is F. B. Perkins' *France under Louis XV* (2 vols., Boston, 1897). Although H. Taine's first volume of his series on the French Revolution entitled *L'ancien régime* (Paris, 1876) and translated as *The Ancient Regime* (translated by John Durand, new revised edition, New York, 1896) has been much criticized for its obvious bias, it contains a mass of interesting detailed information about 18th-century France. Volume VII of the *Cambridge Modern History* (Cambridge, 1909) which deals with the 18th century remains a standard reference.

French Society in the Eighteenth Century by Louis Ducros (translated by W. de Geijer, New York, 1926) is based chiefly on literary sources and deals primarily with the social, and only incidentally with the economic, history of the period. A recent monograph by Elinor Barber entitled *The Bourgeoisie in Eighteenth Century France* (Cambridge, Mass., 1955) makes an interesting attempt to apply modern sociological concepts to eighteenth-century France with provocative, if inconclusive, results.

An older more specialized work, earlier portions of which bear on this problem, is *The Fall of Feudalism in France* (London, 1921) by S. J. Herbert. A more recent excellent study, and relevant in its entirety is Douglas Dakin's *Turgot and the Ancient Regime in France* (London, 1939). American students are fortunate in having accessible one of the most famous of our primary sources for the Old Regime, Arthur Young's *Travels in France during the Years 1787, 1788, 1789,* available in several editions, the best being C. Maxwell's (Cambridge, England, 1929). Although criticized by French scholars for his tendency to compare almost everything in France unfavorably to England, Young's account remains our single most valuable traveler's report of actual observed conditions.

As soon as one begins to move into the area of works in French on the Old Regime it is necessary, for purposes of a bibliography on this scale, to be highly selective. Since it is assumed that those students who do read French probably do so only with some difficulty, only a few of the works most directly relevant to the problem will be cited.

All students who can should become acquainted with relevant portions of the first volume of J. Jaurès' *Histoire Socialiste de la Révolution française* (new edition by Albert Mathiez, 8 vols., Paris, 1922–4). It was in many respects the pioneering work in the area of this problem in that it attempted a systematic and "scientific" analysis of the society and economy of the Old Regime. Besides the important contemporary works of Labrousse and Lefebvre of which portions have been included in the foregoing text, there are also the monumental preliminary studies of these authors: Labrousse's *Esquisse du mouvement des prix et des revenus en France au XVIIIe siècle* (2 vols., Paris, 1933) and Lefebvre's *Les paysans du nord pendant la Révolution française* (Lille, 1924). Only the early sections of the latter deal with conditions during the Old Regime. Lefebvre has also written a great many articles, the most useful of which for the student would be probably a long review article of the Labrousse work mentioned above entitled "Le mouvement des prix et les origines de la Révolution française" which appeared in the *Annales Historiques de la Révolution française* in 1937, and one entitled "Répartition de la propriété et de l'exploitation foncière à la fin de l'ancien régime" which appeared in the *Revue d'histoire moderne* in 1928. Both are reprinted in the collection of Lefebvre's writings entitled *Études sur la Révolution française* (Paris, 1954).

Several older treatments of social and economic aspects of the Old Regime such as A. Aulard's *La Révolution française et le régime féodal* (Paris, 1919); A. Babeau's *La vie rurale sous l'ancien régime* (Paris, 1882) and *Les bourgeois d'autrefois* (Paris, 1886); Loutchisky's *L'état des classes agricoles en France sur la veille de la Révolution* (Paris, 1911); and E. Lavasseur's *Histoire des classes ouvrierès avant 1789* (2 vols. Paris, 1901) are still very useful. Philip Sagnac's recent study of the society of the Old Regime entitled *La formation de la société française moderne* (2 vols., Paris, 1945–6) is a model of its kind.

In his study of all aspects of pre-Revolutionary France the student will find Marcel Marion's *Dictionnaire des institutions de la France aux XVIIe et XVIIIe siècles* (Paris, 1923) an invaluable aid.